"As a Sunday school teacher, I have found this book to be extremely helpful. It is easy to use, fun, and kid-tested! My class can't wait to see which object lesson we'll be using next—and neither can I!"

Rebekah Hamrick, editor, *Teen Light* magazine

"*Ready, Set, Go!* is a dynamic collection of heart-to-heart life lessons built upon the Scriptures. The lessons are fresh, insightful, and easy to adapt due to their uncomplicated structure. This book serves as a great idea springboard; it will help propel any children's ministry beyond the ordinary Sunday school coloring sheet universe."

Angie Rose, children's pastor, Way of Life Haven Center, editor of Christian Children's Book News

"Equipped with easy-to-implement sermons and child-friendly applications, *Ready, Set, Go!* facilitates effective children's ministry. Sermons offer fun, affordable approaches to diverse themes, holidays, and events and are easily adaptable by small and large churches. Both skittish and experienced teachers will appreciate turning to *Ready, Set, Go!* again and again for timeless, life-changing activities."

Lisa A. Crayton, writer, editor of Spirit-Led Writer, and ordained minister

"This insightful book will help teachers share spiritual truths with young children at a level they will understand. It is filled with wonderful lessons and activities and will help anyone who is apprehensive about teaching or in need of creative ideas."

Tammi M. Peters, principal, Fayetteville Christian School

"*Ready, Set, Go!* is a practical, down-to-earth guide for those who serve in children's ministry. It is packed with easy-to-do object lessons that entertain, challenge, and instruct children in how to lead a Christlike life. Adults may just learn a few things along the way too."

Molly Utley, librarian, Hope Mills, North Carolina

"The book is a special gift from God through his servants Annette and Lynn. Both the content and the intent of the lessons will bless children and congregations. There is as much significance to the adults as there will be to the intended audience—children. I thank God that they have taken the time to produce this treasure."

Dr. Tryon D. Lancaster, Methodist College

"Ready, Set, Go! is the perfect resource for any children's pastor. Full-time and lay pastors alike can put this book to immediate use. Enduring truths laid out in simple object lessons. From prayer and preparation to teaching and touching young lives, it's all here in an easy-to-follow format! You'll never say 'I can't' again!"

Dan DeBruler, WCLN 107.3, Christian Listening Network, Fayetteville, North Carolina

"These object lessons will give new ideas and inspiration to children's ministers as they entertain and enlighten children about God. The lessons are simply done but pack a powerful punch in getting the message across. The authors have done a commendable job."

Hazel King, Heritage Bible College

"A delightful collection of thought-provoking sermons for both children and adults. The text is stimulating, well-organized, and will serve as a tremendous help to anyone teaching children's church or Sunday school."

Melinda S. Cooper, Laurens, South Carolina

"Succinct, well-organized, thought-provoking, adaptable, and brilliant."

Ann Stockman, retired teacher

"Annette and Lynn have expressed their love for children in a timeless book that will teach them and their parents throughout the ages."

Ray Lammers, minister

"This book gives you the foundation and basics but allows you the freedom to express your sermon in your own way. It's biblically sound, and the lessons are practical and real to life. These lessons are the ones our children need to hear and will create excitement about learning about the Bible."

R. Gene Hales, Ed.D., superintendent, Clinton City Schools, North Carolina

"The plans for the children's sermons are creative, easy to use, and applicable to children's everyday lives."

Janet Bickel, minister to families with children, Asbury UMC, Raleigh, North Carolina

Ready, Set, Go!

ONE YEAR OF OBJECT LESSONS FOR KIDS

Annette Godwin Dammer

with Lynn Fisher Atchley

 Baker Books

A Division of Baker Book House Co
Grand Rapids, Michigan 49516

© 2003 by Annette Godwin Dammer

Published by Baker Books
a division of Baker Book House Company
P.O. Box 6287, Grand Rapids, MI 49516-6287
www.bakerbooks.com

Printed in the United States of America

Library of Congress Cataloging-in-Publication Data
Dammer, Annette Godwin, 1963–
       Ready, set, go! : one year of object lessons for kids / Annette Godwin Dammer with Lynn Fisher Atchley.
             p.   cm.
       Includes indexes.
       ISBN 0-8010-6444-9
       1. Children's sermons. 2. Sermons, American—20th century. I. Atchley, Lynn Fisher. II. Title.
       BV4315 .D312 2003
       252′.53—dc21   2002153410

To
God, who never put me last,
my husband for unfailing faith through tough times,
the Sweet Boys for hugs that heal,
our parents for backbone and "giggles,"
Myra for prayers and coffee-cup dreamin',
Bruce for faith *and* works,
and the Lammers for the opportunity to minister.
I needed all of you,
for it takes a village to raise an idiot—
uh, I mean a child.
And I am that!
God gave me the very best—you—
and I am grateful!

—Annette

To
my wonderful husband, Sam,
our dear daughters, Katie and Sarah,
my loving family (here and in glory),
my Tabor Church family,
my friends at Fayetteville Christian School,
all my love and appreciation.
And to my heavenly Father,
all honor and glory.

—Lynn

contents

The Point of It All

Lynn and I were teachers at a Christian high school when she shared that she too was a lay children's pastor, and she too worried when she had to write a new sermon. I was comforted to know that other children's pastors needed the same assurances.

I worked on *Ready, Set, Go!* for years but desperately needed a partner in rhyme, an encourager to help O-me-of-little-faith complete the project. I needed Lynn.

Now we hope to join with you in the same way. If God, your Father, has called you to do children's sermons, he will equip you, because he wants the job done well. Remember, Moses wasn't the most confident guy in the world, either.

God is looking for someone who needs to depend on him. My pastor says "nerves" are a good sign. If I ever feel too confident about teaching, too self-assured, that is probably a bad sign.

Spending time in prayer helps me get over being scared about teaching a learned congregation. Prayer reminds me that God has me covered.

I know, because I often ask, "Do I look nervous up there?" And no matter who I ask, they always look shocked and say the same thing: "You just look so comfortable, like you're having sooo much fun!"

And I think, *Thank you, Jesus, for strong anti-perspirant!* No kidding. I realize that the moment I need God, he takes over the pulpit (and the puppet!). Often I can't even remember exactly what I've said. Two weeks later it is completely gone from my mind. When I realized this, I was assured of three things.

1. I needed to write these lessons down to share. They would be useful to others.
2. God doesn't give gifts to be wasted.
3. These are completely God's gifts—or I would be able to recreate them—at least remember them.

So here they are—the gifts Lynn and I were given. We're just passing them along. We know your Father wants you to have them. I truly wish I could hear your version of these sermons. I'd love to hear what new twist God will place on these old words.

The final lesson here is that these lessons are for us as teachers as much as they are for the children. Therefore, we must be as children. We must search and read and study and rest in God's loving words. And God will teach us more—day after day after day, as long as we are willing to hear him. Amen!

Objects

Bag or Basket: Find a large, bright bag or pretty basket in which to bring your "stuff" each week. The kids will get excited when they see it. They find routine very comforting.

Bible Bob the Puppet: Bob can be a simple paper-bag or sock puppet or something more elaborate. You can also use puppet making as a project for the kids in vacation Bible school, Sunday school, or elsewhere. We've made puppets from cute stuffed animals. Make a quick cut along the bottom, remove a bit of the stuffing, and sew in an old sock. Voila!

Being Bob takes practice. Work with him until he becomes a person to you. Develop trademark sounds with your Bob. The kids will come to love and expect those sounds—even the gross ones! Our Bob is rude and immature—a "reverse" role model. I try to be tolerant, but I have my limits! I leave Bob in my bedroom, mouth agape. When I'm in the mood, I talk to Bob and practice sounds and voices. It's a great way to kill stress!

Watching a Muppet or other puppet movie borrowed from your public library will help you find Bob's "voice" for the future.

Ready, Set, Go!

Normally I don't like to be laughed at, because it makes me very uncomfortable. But each of these sermons brought giggles from the pews and a few teary eyes as well. These reactions still shock me just a bit, but they also have caused me to realize that the messages impact children and adults alike. As Christ said, we must *all* be "as a child." So Lynn and I teach in knock-knock (and he shall answer) jokes, dim the lights, sing songs, and use whatever it takes to wake up the pews. My favorite saying is "You can't reach a sleeper." To wake people up, we teach as Christ did—with stories and symbolic objects, such as "planks," "seeds," and "lights." Christ understood how his children learn. He knows we all love a good story. Here Lynn and I try to follow Christ's example.

We hope you'll take the time to meditate and pray on the selected verses. The sermons are short and easy, but what you add to each message is critical. Preparation is essential if you want to be effective. Feel free to add your own experiences and your own objects. Current events or holidays may inspire a change. Depending on your learning style and personality, you may want to memorize the sermons or merely get the gist of them, pray, and go. Both techniques work well. Find God's will for *you*.

For clarity (always important to the nervous and rushed servant!), we have utilized the succinct organization modeled in *Object Lessons about God* by Kyle Godfrey. Each sermon is organized as follows:

The Point of It All—a quick summary

Objects—what you'll need to collect

To Dos—preparation list that includes a list of "accomplices" to involve ahead of time, so they aren't caught off guard

Ready, Set, Go!—the sermon itself, with stage directions in parentheses

With every section, change what you need to change. I used to practice my sermons in front of my own children or my husband. I asked them to listen—and to interrupt often. Then I quizzed them on the sermon to see if I had gotten my point across.

Children will alter your lesson as you go—that is, they will interrupt. Expect it. Accept it. Grow comfortable with who God made children to be. Keeping the children and their parents comfortable and coming back is much more important than one day's message. God will make sure they hear what they need to hear.

Fighting the flow is very stressful, restrictive, and painful for all involved—parents especially. You'll rarely win the battle anyway. Kids with an audience are highly motivated. They aren't bad; they are just performers at heart. Encourage them to be polite, but encourage them. They may be willing to sit in your spot one day.

Finally, instructions for craft or class ideas are included with pertinent lessons. These crafts can be duplicated by the kids in children's church or Sunday school. The activities will mirror and reinforce the lesson for all.

If you need us, contact us through our magazine, *Teen Light*, at http://www.teenlight.org or email Annette at annette@teenlight.org. We'd love to know how you're doing.

Ready? Set? You said, "Send me!" Now God has. Go! You can do it!

PART 1

Special Events and Holidays

Valentine's Day

The Point of It All

Sometimes we try to win God's love. We forget that he loves us no matter what. He has already given us the ultimate Valentine—his Son—and sends sweet cards each day to remind us of that undying love.

Objects

A valentine or two

Something representing Easter—a cross, if possible

To Dos

Reflect on your motive for this ministry. Are you trying to prove your worth to God? He already knows how wonderful you are. Trust in that.

Verses to Pray On

1 John 4:8

He who does not love does not know God, for God is love.

1 John 4:10

*In this is love, not that we loved God,
but that He loved us and sent His Son
to be the propitiation for our sins.*

1 John 4:19

We love Him because He first loved us.

Ready, Set, Go!

What a special week this is with Valentine's Day coming up. What is your favorite Valentine's gift to get? *(Pause.)* What do you give on Valentine's Day? *(Pause.)*

What if day after day you sent someone a valentine, and that person never sent one back? How would you feel? What if that person never even opened it to read it?

Do you want to hear something sad? People do that to God every day. He sends them sunrises and sunsets, beautiful flowers and green grass, friends and family to love them. Yet they never even realize that those wonderful gifts are from God to them. And they rarely say thank you!

Now, in a month or so, we will celebrate God's greatest gift, the gift of his Son. You know, Easter! Think about this—who is the gift for? *(Pause.)* That's right. You and me. Is it just for people who pray and go to church? *(Pause.)* No. Isn't that amazing? God made that sacrifice for everybody. There are people around us who don't even believe God exists. But some of them will someday. Others won't believe in God until the day they die. Nevertheless, Jesus died on the cross so we might all have a chance to be saved—every one of us.

God loves us that much. He loved us even before we loved him. The Bible says we love God because he first loved us. His love teaches us how to love, and we do our best to love him back and to love his other children.

No matter what, God loves us. He keeps sending his valentines, even if people who don't believe in God never accept the cross, never accept that Jesus had to die for their sins. He keeps sending his valentines, even if they never see Jesus' death as an act of love that God knew we needed.

God and his Son, Jesus, knew what we needed to live, and they gave it to us two thousand years ago—long before any of us were born. What a blessing! What a true gift of love!

Let's pray. *(Ask a child to pray or use the following.)* Father, it hurts to think what you had to do for us, but I know you know best. And I know you love us. You showed us by sending us your Son. It is a gift we need if we are to come home to you in heaven someday. Thank you. Help those of us still hurting to find peace with your loving sacrifice. Thanks for loving me before I even knew you! Amen.

If You Were Your Very, Very Best, Jesus Still Would Have Died

Palm Sunday

The Point of It All

It is difficult to imagine the pain Christ endured. He paid the penalty for our sin—ours and all of humanity—on the cross because of his love for us. Because some people have never experienced selfless, giving love, it is hard for them to understand the love of Christ.

Objects

Use any of the items below that you may find around your house. Hold them up as you ad lib about them.

Things that represent what Christ went through in the days before his crucifixion—for example, a cross, a sword, or a whip

Objects that represent how we care for our kids

Objects that a child may damage—a single sock (its mate apparently lost or torn), a pair of sneakers, a stained T-shirt, a broken toy

Something a child or adult might covet—an ad for a Mercedes or a boat

A ticket to heaven—make one or bring a ticket you may have at home

To Dos

Gather your supplies in a nice basket.

Relax and pray about your own feelings about Easter. God knew from the beginning that humanity would sin, and he planned to deal with our guilt and sin once and for all on the cross—all because of his love for us. We will never be perfect this side of heaven, but we rest in the assurance that God provides grace for every one of us.

Verses to Pray On

Luke 15:7

I say to you that likewise there will be more joy in heaven over one sinner who repents than over ninety-nine just persons who need no repentance.

Romans 3:22–25

For there is no difference; for all have sinned
and fall short of the glory of God, being justified freely
by His grace through the redemption
that is in Christ Jesus.

Ready, Set, Go!

We're coming up on my favorite time of year—Easter! But I didn't always feel that way. Do you know why? Do you know what Jesus went through during this week? *(Pause.)*

That's right, he was betrayed by a friend, beaten with whips, and hung on a cross. And he never did a bad thing in his life. Not one! But now he lives. And that's what *next* Sunday is all about. His Father brought him back to life so that all who trust in him may live in heaven together someday.

Now that is beautiful, isn't it? Worth it all. Jesus and his dad, God, love us very, very much. They knew what we needed, just like your parents always seem to know what you need—a good dinner, clothes, a bed to sleep in. They take care of you so you can be happy.

But sometimes I think, *If only I could be good, Jesus wouldn't have had to die like that.* Then, for a while, I'll try to be perfect. But then I mess up—about once every five minutes. *(Smile and cross your eyes.)* You know—I want someone else's car, feel jealous because they have so much stuff, or get mad over nothing at all. Then I get very angry with myself. Do you ever do things like that? Do you say things you don't mean or think mean thoughts? *(Pause for examples.)*

On my good days, I try hard. But I still mess up. My best, my very best, is not perfect. I hate to even say it, but it's so. And God knows that—just like moms and dads know kids

23

will wear out sneakers and break glasses and mess up their bedrooms. On those good days, I try to forgive myself. I fix whatever went wrong and try to figure out why so I won't just keep doing it over and over again. But that's the best I can do. I might still mess up that very thing again. And God knows that too, even before I do!

But God the Father loves me anyway. And so does Jesus. And that's why they planned Easter. That's why Jesus chose to die on the cross, even though he knew it would be the hardest day of his life.

So what is my point this Palm Sunday? Christ suffered. He died a horrible death on the cross, even though he was innocent. He never did even *one* thing wrong. He died because he loved us so much.

And whether you accept the gift of God's love or not, he already gave it—two thousand years ago. God loved us so much that he gave us his Son. If we do accept the gift of God's love, we also receive the wonderful gift of a ticket to heaven! Our heavenly Father, and his Son, Jesus, want me—and you—and you *(point to each of them, maybe some parents too)* to come and live with them forever. They love us that much!

Let's pray. *(Ask a child to pray, or use the following.)* Father, what a gift. On days when I feel gloomy, help me to focus on your love. Help me to feel that love and share it with someone else. You love me and all those I love. And you want us all to be together with you and your Son in heaven. Thank you! Amen.

Easter Eggs
Hunt for Treasure

The Point of It All

Jesus lives! And he loves us! That *is* something to celebrate!

Objects

Enough empty plastic Easter eggs for each child (arranged in a basket)

A basketful of candy, or treats to toss or hand around

To Dos

Arrange the plastic eggs in a basket. Dress them up so the kids "crave" the eggs.

Hide the candy or treats under the eggs, or in another basket to place behind where you'll stand to teach.

Verses to Pray On

John 20:15

Woman, why are you weeping? Whom are you seeking?

John 20:19

Peace be with you.

John 20:21

So Jesus said to them again, "Peace to you! As the Father has sent Me, I also send you."

Ready, Set, Go!

The big day—Easter—is finally here! Christ is risen! Let's hear a cheer. "Jesus lives today! Hip, hip, hooray! Jesus lives today! Hip, hip, hooray!" *(Walk them through it; motion to the parents to join in.)* Jesus lives today! Hip, hip, hooray! *(Repeat a couple of times.)*

Wow! Jesus lives. And lives. And lives. But when he died, his friends, those who loved him, were very, very sad. And they buried him—very dead indeed—in a tomb with a large stone for a door. And they cried. They did not know Jesus would live again.

But they were in for a surprise, weren't they?

Speaking of surprises, would you like a prize egg? (Pass them out.) Open your eggs now. On three. One, two, three! Do you like my gift? *(Pause.)* What do you mean they're empty? Let me see. *(Pause, then smile.)* I know, they're empty. Were you surprised?

Can you imagine how Mary Magdalene, a friend of Jesus, felt when she went to his tomb, found the huge boulder moved away from the opening, and saw that the grave was empty? She certainly was not expecting that! And she wasn't happy about it. In fact, she began to cry. She thought someone had stolen Jesus' dead body.

But Jesus was right behind her. *(Pass out the "real" treats—from behind you, if possible.)* It was a glorious surprise for all those who loved Jesus. It was such a surprise that some people don't even believe it! *(Shake your head in disbelief.)*

But you and I believe what God did. And we're all blessed by Jesus' life. So Easter *is* a day to rejoice, isn't it?

Jesus lives! Jesus lives! We will have many more surprises—and even questions—as we move along life's road. But we need to remember that Jesus *is* alive. And the treat—heaven—is guaranteed for those who believe.

And there's more: love and peace and the company and comfort of the Holy Spirit.

Let's cheer one more time. Parents, help us out *(motion to the pews)*. "Jesus lives today! Hip, hip, hooray! Jesus lives today! Hip, hip, hooray!"

Let's pray. *(Ask a child to pray or use the following.)* Father, the gifts you give are enormous, and we are sooo grateful. Thank you Father God, and thank you Jesus, for loving us so very, very much. What a gift! Amen.

Mother's Day Gifts

The Point of It All

Moms are God's gifts to all of us.

Objects

A bundle of flowers

If you have a small church, bring a flower for every mom. At least try to have one for the newest mom in your church, the mom with the most children, the pastor's wife, and so on. You may want to add a gift for your own mom. This is one day your friends won't mind if you play favorites! Let the kids make the deliveries. If you can't give flowers, substitute something else such as a cake after church or a baggie of inexpensive chocolate candies tied with a teabag for each mother. The kids could write a verse the week before on squares of construction paper. Let them attach their cards with teabags, twist ties, or pipe cleaners.

To Dos

Treat yourself to one of God's gifts—perhaps a sunset with an iced tea and lemon.

Why not pray and then write your own mom a note thanking her for the good gifts she gave you. Even the "toughest" mom may have imparted a sense of humor, strength, or some other character quality. If your mom has passed on or isn't in your life, you might want to write to someone who was a mom to you—even if that was your dad! If you can't write the note, try journaling about it.

Verses to Pray On

John 19:25–28, 30

Now there stood by the cross of Jesus His mother, and His mother's sister, Mary the wife of Clopas, and Mary Magdalene. When Jesus therefore saw His mother, and the disciple whom He loved standing by, He said to His mother, "Woman, behold your son!" Then He said to the disciple, "Behold your mother!" And from that hour that disciple took her to his own home. After this, Jesus, knowing that all things were now accomplished, that the Scripture might be fulfilled, said, "I thirst!" . . . So when Jesus had received the sour wine, He said, "It is finished!" And bowing His head, He gave up His spirit.

Ready, Set, Go!

I want to thank all of the moms that brought you here today. Did you know that without your mom you wouldn't even be here on earth? That's something to think about, isn't it? *(Pause.)* When you add in all the meals and washed clothes and hugs and kisses and cuddles during stormy nights—well, we're pretty blessed, aren't we?

Sometimes in my life, I've even been blessed with a special aunt or teacher who felt like a mom. *(Who can you share about? Mother's Day and Father's Day are really tough for some kids. What could you say today that would really minister to them?)* I was grateful God sent them too. God always knows whom I need.

In fact, God is always showing how much he loves us. He sends people to love and care for us. He sends us a sunrise and a sunset *every day.* He surrounds us with beautiful flowers. How can we share God's love? *(Pause.)*

I have an idea! What if we thank our moms—and those who love us like a mom—by sharing God's love? One clear night next week, make a date with your special person. Take a blanket outside and share the stars and the moon with them. Pick some lovely flowers from a field or make a card. Make your bed. Imagine that! *(Laugh and roll your eyes.)* Use your allowance to buy a flower or a candy bar. God shows us his love, and he wants us to share it!

Our moms share God's love every day. This day—and all week long—we need to thank them. Let them know we appreciate all the school play costumes, all the homework help, every meal they cook after a hard day, and on and on. And thank God for them too!

So bring Mom a cup of juice and watch a sunrise with her. Offer to set the table and make her promise to spend that five minutes sitting down to watch a sunset alone with her Bible.

Share God's gifts with those you love. And share yourself, because God made you too.

Let's pray. *(Ask a child to pray or use the following.)* Father, you make it clear day after day how much you love us. Help me remember to share your love. Amen.

To the Pastor's Wife

The Point of It All

We all have birthdays, even Jesus. But his *death* is what lets us live! Living forever with him is the greatest gift of all.

Objects

A birthday cake—best if a surprise
Candles and a match
Any party favors you have left over from a past event
Flowers, cards, or bookmarks made by the children in Sunday school. The theme could be: "You're important to us because . . ."

To Dos

Bake or purchase a family-sized birthday cake.
Gather birthday items and hide them near the pulpit.
Get an accomplice to dim the lights, light the cake, and take it to your pastor's wife.
Assign an older child to deliver any flowers, gifts, or cards.

Verses to Pray On

Luke 22:19

This is My body which is given for you.

Luke 24:46–48

Thus it is written, and thus it was necessary for the Christ to suffer and to rise from the dead the third day, and that repentance and remission of sins should be preached in His name to all nations, beginning at Jerusalem. And you are witnesses of these things.

Ready, Set, Go!

Did you guys know that today is Mrs. _____'s birthday? *(Pause.)* That's exciting, isn't it? Let's sing "Happy Birthday." One, two, three! *(Sing. You may want to add a verse that says, "God's blessings to you, God's blessings to you, God's blessings dear _____, God's blessings to you!" During the singing your helpers should deliver the cake and gifts and dim the lights. Your pastor's wife should blow out the candles. She may take the cake home, unless you want to plan a cake and coffee party after church.)*

How many of you have birthdays? Me too! Everybody does. They're great to celebrate, aren't they? I love birthdays!

How many of you celebrate death? Oewww! Huh?

But there is one person who died for us. Without him we'd be in a mess. Who is that? *(Pause.)*

That's right! Jesus Christ. Let's remember him today. His death is a glorious gift, and he gave that gift so we can live with him forever. Praise God that part of his plan—an important part—is that Jesus rose from the dead and now lives! Today! We have a lot to celebrate, don't we? Let's give one more big "Happy Birthday" to Mrs. _____. Ready? One, two, three! Happy Birthday!

Let's pray. *(Ask a child to pray or use the following.)* Father God, thank you for your gifts to us. Sweet Jesus, thank you for giving us life. And thank you, Father, for Mrs. _____.

31

She's such a blessing to us for so many reasons. *(Feel free to add them.)* Amen.

Father's Day

The Point of It All

We all can celebrate Father's Day. We share the greatest Dad of all!

Objects

Child's plastic fishing rod

Lightweight doll, like a small Raggedy Andy, or make one from paper or a magazine picture—the floppier the better

Bible with bookmark at Matthew 6:9–13

To Dos

Tie doll to end of fishing rod.

Practice casting the doll with the rod.

Verses to Pray On

Matthew 6:9–13

The Lord's Prayer and the surrounding verses in which Christ calls God "your Father."

Ready, Set, Go!

Hi, guys! Having a great day? *(Pause.)* It's so good to see all of you! Do you know what today is? *(Pause.)* That's right, Father's Day! Why do we celebrate Father's Day? *(Pause.)*

Good answer! We want to celebrate our dads, because they love us and take care of us and because we love them too, right?

And they do stuff with us, like fish or even cook. *(Here's a great place to tell a Dad or other "great guy" story of your own.)*

Did you know that God is your Father too? We say a prayer in church that starts out that way. You know it. Our Father, who . . . *(pause for them to add on; wave your hand in a "Follow me!" gesture)* art in heaven. That's right!

Jesus taught us those words as a great way to pray. In fact, near that passage Jesus calls God "your Father" *(point to several of the verses)* eleven times!

And God *is* your Father. Mine too. And your mom and dad's Father! Amazing, isn't it? So, what do we give God on this Father's Day? He has everything, you know. Everything belongs to him. Hmmm.

Well, how about if *(whip out fishing pole with doll dangling from it; cast it out and reel it in)* we *do* something for God on Father's Day? *(Cast out and reel in.)* What if we become "fishers of men," just like he asked?

What if we tell others about how our Father God loves us and takes care of us? What if we tell our friends that we love God and why? *(Cast out and reel in.)* What if we tell them about the things our Father God does for us, even when we're *(wave pole and doll around again)* fishing . . . for men!

Let's pray. *(Ask a child to pray or use the following.)* Thank you, Father God. You love and care for us and send dads and grandfathers to love us too. And thanks for taking us fishing! Amen.

RSVP to VBS

The Point of It All

Who can I invite to Vacation Bible School? Which kids might be left out? Can I offer to drive them to VBS and give their parents a few hours of rest?

Objects

VBS invitations

To Dos

Make and copy invitations. Make enough copies for members of the congregation to share with friends and neighbors.

If your church is large, you may want older kids with invitations stationed around the church so that passing them out doesn't take so long. You may want to leave even more invitations by the door.

Pray for the children who need to come. How can you get them to VBS with no strings or expectations attached? A seed planted today may sprout in twenty years—but sprout it will!

Verses to Pray On

Matthew 21:14–16

Then the blind and the lame came to Him in the temple, and He healed them. But when the chief priests and scribes saw the wonderful things that He did, and the chil-

dren crying out in the temple and saying, "Hosanna to the Son of David!" they were indignant and said to Him, "Do You hear what these children are saying?" And Jesus said to them, "Yes. Have you never read, 'Out of the mouth of babes and nursing infants You have perfected praise?'"

Ready, Set, Go!

Thank you for coming! *(Pause. Remember to make eye contact with as many children as possible. Focus on these sets of eager eyes one at a time. We all need to feel important.)* Do you know something? There are kids right here in our community whose parents don't come to church. So the kids don't get to come either. They don't get to know Jesus, sing, or come to Vacation Bible School, or any other great events we have. And they don't have the fun of getting to know *you!*

But guess what! You can bring them here. When friends spend the night with you, bring them. Or just invite them to church once in a while. Ask Mom or Dad if it's OK to pick them up on the way. It doesn't have to be every Sunday.

Make them feel welcome. Needed. Wanted.

Did you ever know somebody who was having a party but didn't invite you? Maybe you couldn't get a ride or had other plans. Maybe you weren't sure you even wanted to go. But you still wanted to be invited. To be included. To be welcome.

That's how it is for everybody. Maybe the only reason you weren't invited was because they thought you wouldn't come. Maybe you weren't invited because you *did* have plans. Either way, it hurt not to be invited, didn't it?

Here is a solution. I have a great big stack of invitations to our Vacation Bible School. VBS will be here, at the church, from _____ to _____. The information is

35

on the invitations. All you have to do is pass them out—here, there, everywhere your parents suggest. It's a great way to meet your neighbors. When your new friends come to VBS, we can make them feel welcome, wanted, and loved.

OK, everyone take a pile. Anybody in the pews up to a little missions work? If you want some, please raise your hand. Our young ambassadors for Christ here *(point to the kids and smile proudly)* will be glad to deliver as many invitations as you need. *(Urge kids to deliver the invitations around the pews. They should leave a few near the exit for the shy.)* Please help us. There are many seeds to plant, many children who are waiting just to be asked.

While the kids pass out the invitations, let's pray over our VBS. *(Ask a child to pray or use the following.)* Father, there are so many lonely children, single mothers who need a break, unchurched, and discouraged neighbors. If we only plant one seed, let it be fruitful. Let us share the welcoming love and light of your church with our neighbors. Make us bold as we go forth. Help us hand over any fear of rejection to you. Amen.

Thanks kids! What a blessing you are! And thanks to those in the pews who bring you here. We *all* need to feel welcome and needed. Thank you.

Are You Grounded?

for VBS or a Special Service

The Point of It All

How deep are we planted? Are we easy to pluck up, or choked by worry?

Objects

Bible with bookmark at Luke 8

Bird/devil face (see below)

Two trees (see below)

Sheet of red construction paper, marking pen, scissors, tape, newspapers (for devil and trees)

To Dos

Make bird/devil face (see below).

Make two growing trees (see below).

Pray about the things that pluck your focus or your faith away. What chokes your walk or the purity of your thoughts? Does fear ever affect you? How do you fight it?

Verses to Pray On

Luke 8:5–18

Jesus' parable of the sower.

Ready, Set, Go!

It is so good to see you again! We've talked before about how Jesus taught with stories. Remember? We call them parables, but they are just stories that help us learn and remember Jesus' lessons. When Jesus was traveling with his twelve disciples, people came from every city to hear him. The story is in your Bibles in Luke 8. *(Raise Bible.)* There Jesus tells a parable about a man who planted, or sowed *(motion seed throwing)*, seeds. Have any of you ever planted seeds? *(Pause.)*

Well, this man went out to sow his seeds *(motion sowing)*. As he sowed, some fell by the side and were trampled, and the birds swooped down and ate them all up. *(Have red paper bird swoop down. Stop and look at the kids to make your point.)* Mmm-mmm, delicious! For the bird, that is!

Some of those seeds fell on the rocks, sprang right up, but then withered away because they had no water. *(While telling this, stretch paper tree out a bit and gently push it back down.)*

Other seeds fell among thorny, prickly old plants. The seeds grew, but those thorny, prickly plants grew too. *(Again, make tree grow, higher this time, then slowly lower with a choking/gagging noise.)* Well, the thorns took over, choking the good plants. *(Stick out your tongue and choke. Then smile.)*

Finally, there was one last group. These seeds fell on good ground. They sprang up and grew *(stretch and stretch tree as you talk)* and grew and *grew!* And those plants gave a crop one hundred times bigger than the seeds they came from. Imagine one hundred times what you planted. That's very good, isn't it?

Now when Jesus finished telling this story, he said loudly, "He who has ears to hear, let him hear!" OK, who has ears to hear? Show them to me! *(Pull on your own ears and waggle your head. Hopefully they will copy you.)*

Plants? Birds? Seeds? His disciples were puzzled. What was Jesus talking about? So they asked him. And Jesus said, "To you it has been given to know the mysteries of the kingdom of God, but to the rest it is given in parables, that 'Seeing they may not see, and hearing they may not understand'" (Luke 8:10). In other words, you and I will understand it, but those who don't love God won't get it.

So Jesus explained that the seed is the Word of God. Those by the side of the road are people who hear God's Word, but then the devil comes *(swoop bird again)* and snatches that Word right out of their hearts just to make sure they won't "believe and be saved." Scary stuff! *(At this point open the red bird to show scary devil face inside. Crumple paper and throw it over your shoulder with a shudder.)*

The people on the rocks are those who hear and are excited at first. But their faith never takes root, never goes deep. They believe for a while and then, in a time of temptation, fall away. *(Extend the second tree about halfway.)*

Remember the seeds that fell in the thorny bush? Those seeds, or words of God, are heard but are choked out *(stretch the tree and choke again)* by fear, worries, money, and pleasures. The people who at first receive the Word of God have no time for him.

Now the other seeds landed on good ground. These people hear God's Word with a noble and good heart. They keep God's Word and bear fruit with patience. *(Make tree grow to its fullest and shake it joyfully. Smile big!)*

So what do we need to do? We need to make sure our hearts are good ground by reading our Bibles and praying and coming to church in healthy groups of friends and family. And we need ears to hear. *(Wiggle ears again.)* Come on, wiggle those ears!

Let's pray. *(Ask a child to pray or use the following.)* Father, if we're strangled by fear, if we forget what you've taught us, or if we've stopped taking your love and promises to heart, help us, Father. Move us to where we can grow. Give us ears to hear. Thanks for always loving us enough to want us to grow and bear fruit. Amen.

Directions for Bird/Devil Face

Fold a piece of red construction paper in half. Cut like bird in figure 1. Draw a bird's eye. Open and lay paper flat so that the bird's eye is on the backside. On the inside, draw the devil's face as in figure 2.

Figure 1   Figure 2

Directions for Growing Tree

Make two of these.

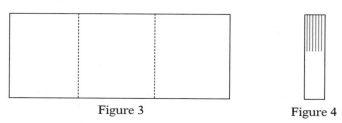

Figure 3   Figure 4

Take three sheets of newspaper and tape them end to end with an inch or two overlap. Dashes are taped areas. Roll lengthwise and tape on side. Use scissors to cut strips one-third of the way down from the top. Cut through all layers as shown in dotted lines on figure 4. Strips may be any width, but 1 to 2 inches works best for nice, fluffy leaves. To make tree "grow," just pull center layer out. Note: These will push back into shape easily if not pulled to full extension. The trees also make great take-home projects for the kids.

fourth of July

freedom All Year Round

The Point of It All

Jesus gave us freedom—from death and laws we're unable to keep.

Objects

Sparklers in pews and "on stage"
Lighters
Pots and pans
Wooden spoons
Patriotic music ("America the Beautiful" or "God Bless America") and a CD or tape player

To Dos

Check with your church/pastor to see if it's OK to light sparklers in the church.

Set up your music. Get a helper if you need one.

Arrange for someone to turn off the lights while the sparklers are burning and to turn them on again on cue. Arrange for sparklers in the audience, horns, or anything festive that celebrates freedom.

Arrange for children (old enough to bang on signal) to hit pots with spoons. You may want to have pot bangers in the pews too.

41

Verses to Pray On

Romans 8:2

For the law of the Spirit of life in Christ Jesus has made me free from the law of sin and death.

Galatians 5:1

Stand fast therefore in the liberty by which Christ has made us free, and do not be entangled again with a yoke of bondage.

Ready, Set, Go!

Welcome, welcome! What special holiday are we celebrating this week? *(Pause.)* Yes, the Fourth of July. I love Independence Day! Does anybody know why we celebrate? *(Pause.)* Yes. We celebrate our nation's freedom.

I love sparklers! And have you ever banged a pot? *(Signal the "clangers.")* Exciting, isn't it? Almost sounds like "the bombs bursting in air!" It's kind of like being back in the American Revolution, when the colonies fought for freedom from England. We didn't want to be bound by laws we didn't make. We wanted *life, freedom. (Signal pot clangers again.)*

But we had to fight for it. Many died for it on both sides.

Before Jesus, people followed lots of rules. They were bound by so many laws that it was impossible to keep them all. They had hundreds of rules to follow at a time—day after day. But doing good things nonstop still didn't make it possible for people to get to heaven.

So God sent his Son to take our punishment on the cross and make us righteous, so that we can be free from sin and ready for heaven. Jesus was the only one who had to die so that we could all live. Free! Free from the laws and free from death. Heaven forever.

42

Now that is freedom, isn't it? Lights out, please. Music, please! Sparklers! Pots and pans! Sing along if you want! *(Pause for song. Encourage the adults to sing with welcoming hand signals.)* Amen! We are free! Lights on, please.

OK, let's pray. *(Ask a child to pray or use the following.)* Father, you have given us great freedom. Help us to remember that and share it—365 days a year. Amen.

Christmas in July

The Point of It All

Christ can get lost in the celebration of Christmas. But we can celebrate his life every day—even today!

Objects

Candles for each singer in the audience and one for you

Matches or lighters

To Dos

Choose a simple, popular Christmas carol (first verse will do).

If possible, practice the carol with an older child or two. Use the older kids as positive role models and helpers. They will help you keep order, and they won't feel like they're doing "baby" stuff.

Get a few helpers in the audience to dim the lights, light their candles, and rise and sing.

Verses to Pray On

Luke 2:7–14

And she brought forth her firstborn Son, and wrapped Him in swaddling cloths, and laid Him in a manger, because there was no room for them in the inn. Now there were in the same country shepherds living out in the fields, keeping watch over their flock by night. And behold, an angel of the Lord stood before them, and the glory of the Lord shone around them, and they were greatly afraid. Then the angel said to them, "Do not be afraid, for behold, I bring you good tidings of great joy which will be to all people. For there is born to you this day in the city of David a Savior, who is Christ the Lord. And this will be the sign to you: You will find a Babe wrapped in swaddling cloths, lying in a manger." And suddenly there was with the angel a multitude of the heavenly host praising God and saying: "Glory to God in the highest, And on earth peace, good will toward men!"

Ready, Set, Go!

(Ask someone to dim the lights just before you head to the front.) Sometimes it can seem dark, can't it? But don't you love Christmas with all the lights? *(Pause.)* Do you remember the shepherds? *(Pause.)* I love the shepherds. I love how God and his angels picked good, faithful servants, not the mighty and famous.

Many of you know that we *celebrate* Christ's birth on December 25, but that his *real* birth had to be on another day. So if we choose to celebrate then, why can't we choose to celebrate other days too? Like today? Or every day?

Not with packages and boxes and bows. I love all that too. But no matter how hard I try, each December 25 my focus is moved off of Christ and his birthday. Every year I try to focus on Jesus, and every year I never quite make it.

So I've decided to celebrate Christ's birthday whenever I need a boost. I sing a Christmas carol or buy one person I love a gift. I celebrate Christ's birth because it is his life and his lessons that make *my* life so happy. It's his birth that will bring my family together in heaven—a true "happily ever after."

Now that's something to sing about! OK, what's your favorite Christmas carol? *(Pick one ahead of time just in case you have a young audience or a variety of strong opinions.)* Let's sing it together. *(Let the children get a round in before you invite the audience to join. Then cue lighting of the candles by lighting your own. Bring "light" into the church. Have your carolers rise and begin to sing. Make sure they turn toward the pews.)*

Ah! I see some light. Let's sing some more. Louder. *(One more verse—the same one over and over is fine. Everyone understands you're working with children.)* All of us. Come on! *(Point to the audience. At the end of the verse, make sure the lights are returned to bright.)*

Let's pray. *(Ask a child to pray or use the following.)* Father, help us celebrate Christ's birth every day with the love, laughter, and freedom you've given us. Help us bring light into our world by celebrating the wonder of you and all you do. Amen.

Back to School

The Point of It All

We should never stop learning. It brings us closer to God and his world and enables us to share this with others.

Objects

Calculator

Videotapes or audiotapes

Cleaning rag, vegetable (carrot), or chunk of wood—
anything representing hard labor around the home

Bible

To Dos

Gather your supplies into a tote or large wicker basket
for easy carrying. The kids will get excited the moment
they see it.

Rest and reflect on how modern science gives us more
time with God. We don't have to haul water or heat it
over hand-chopped wood. We walk away as a machine
does our laundry. Vacuuming involves a few swipes
of the carpet. We don't have to drive an important
document across the country; we just fax or email it.

Reflect on how that saved time could be put to God's
use—extra time with family, prayer and study, spreading the gospel. How could each of us use this gift of
time better? Could I use it to learn something new?
A few greetings in Spanish taped to the kitchen cab-
inet? A new recipe? A new song? A Bible verse? Just
1 thing x 365 days x the years of my life = one good
life.

Verses to Pray On

Proverbs 10:14

Wise people store up knowledge,
But the mouth of the foolish is near destruction.

Proverbs 12:23–24

A prudent man conceals knowledge,
But the heart of fools proclaims foolishness.
The hand of the diligent will rule,
But the slothful will be put to forced labor.

Ecclesiastes 7:19–20

Wisdom strengthens the wise
More than ten rulers of the city.
For there is not a just man on earth who does good
And does not sin.

Ready, Set, Go!

I don't think we should go back to school. What do you think of that? We're getting ready to go back, and all I can think is, "Why?" I mean, why should we bother with school? Isn't it enough to learn about God and be a good person? Why should we waste time learning and going to school? *(Pause for many, many reactions!)*

Take math, for instance. Why should we learn math when we have calculators? *(Wave the items you've brought as you speak about each one.)* And why should we learn to spell when we have spelling checkers on our computers? And reading—how stupid! We have videos and tapes. Why would we need to read? Don't they even have the Bible on tape? And there are tons of Christian cartoon videos we can watch. And we come *here*, don't we?

The way I see it, if kids didn't have to go to school, they could help around the house more. We could go back to chopping wood and save money on our electric bill. We could get rid of the washing machine and all of that wasted water and let you get your workout there—right? Sweeping, carrying, gardening—we would even have time to grow and harvest our own vegetables. *Lots* of them! And with the exercise we'd get picking beans and digging weeds, we wouldn't need P.E. or sports. That would mean no more fees or special shoes.

And we wouldn't need all these cars and gas, because parents wouldn't need to run all over town for all those school festivals and activities and games and stuff. We'd all have much more time to be home, wouldn't we?

But you know me better than that, don't you? I love being home and being with my family, and I wouldn't give up my time alone with my Bible for anything, because that's when God and I sit down and spend time together. And I love to read to my kids. I love it even more when they read to me. Now, I do enjoy listening to books on tape and watching videos for fun. But I love to learn too. We're never too old, you know!

What do God and math have to do with one another? *(Pause.)* How about God and science? *(Pause.)* Well, God created the world, its creatures, everything. Science and math bring us a little closer to understanding it all. English helps us tell about it or to understand what we read. Social studies and history help us see God's people over time— how he's loved them and how they've grown or even failed.

And the more we learn, the more we can change the world. We can become scientists or doctors who care for God's children. We can become caregivers who nurture and teach God's littlest babies. We can learn about paying bills, cooking healthy food, and saving money to help our families live better and longer.

Proverbs 12:24 says that hard workers will rule and the lazy will be *forced* to hard, hard work. Ecclesiastes 7:19 says "Wisdom strengthens the wise more than ten rulers of the city." That means the wise will be stronger than ten rulers! God gave us a brain to use. And using it is a great way to honor him and the miracle of our minds.

Let's pray. *(Ask a child to pray or use the following.)* Father, our brains are a true mystery. You have given each of us talents molded to exactly who we are. Help us to find our gifts and use them. If we are meant to comfort, if we are best at baking, if we are math maniacs, help us to grow—toward you. Amen.

Homecoming

The Point of It All

Our church is a comforting home, and it needs our care and attention.

Objects

Dusting rag or other cleaning materials (easy to carry)
Something cooked or baked for homecoming that's very
  portable and hard to spill

To Dos

Rest and pray.
Enjoy homecoming!

Verse to Pray On

John 14:23

If anyone loves Me, he will keep My word; and My Father will love him, and We will come to him and make Our home with him.

Ready, Set, Go!

(Welcome children, then read John 14:23.) This verse always brings me great comfort. Do you ever get lonely and hug a stuffed animal or ask someone you love for a hug? Do you ever just go to your room for comfort, or come home and take a deep sniff of what's cooking? *(Take a big whiff of air. Make a sniffing noise, or bug out your eyes and say, "Mmm!")* Those things are comforting and make us feel at home.

What do you love most about home? *(Pause.)*

Can you imagine if you didn't have a home? *(Pause.)*

Did you know that this is your church home? It's a blessing to have a church home, isn't it? *(If you've been "church homeless" before, share that loneliness with them.)*

I bet each of you helps out at home, dusts *(hold prop up as you talk)*, works in the kitchen. Those jobs often go unnoticed, don't they? Do you know who took out the garbage or locked the house last night? Did someone pay the electric bill and the phone bill this month? Did you notice?

The funny thing is, when these jobs are done well, nobody notices. In fact, who does those things for our church home? Who came in and turned on the lights and the air conditioning (or heat) today? Who made sure everything was just right for our wonderful meal after this service? Who prepared the drinks, and set out the salt and pepper?

Let's find out, and let's help today. Having a home takes a bit of work. Let's give out hugs of thanks, and pick up empty cups and used napkins from the tables. It's not very glamorous, but it's what makes a building a home. I'll help too.

Let's pray. *(Ask a child to pray or use the following.)* Father, you've given us such a beautiful home and filled it with family. Help us to concretely thank each of your homemakers with a smile or a hug, because we all need to be cared for and appreciated. Bless each of us with peace and love. Amen.

Clergy/Pastor Appreciation Week

The Point of It All

We need to build up our pastors and let them know they make a difference in our lives.

Objects

Card or letter from you to your pastor telling what you appreciate about him or her

Cards or letters from the kids (if you can arrange it through Sunday school)

Basket or bag of home-baked goodies, or some small gift for your pastor(s) and assistants

To Dos

Organize the above (bake muffins or some other treat).

Try to enlist Sunday school teachers or parents in making/purchasing gifts.

Prepare a child to deliver the gifts so there isn't a last minute scuffle for the privilege.

Prepare a couple of older children to compliment the pastor. (Impromptu is better, more heartfelt, but if you surprise the children, they may surprise you by not saying anything.)

51

Verses to Pray On

Romans 14:19

Therefore let us pursue the things which make for peace and the things by which one may edify another.

Hebrews 10:24

And let us consider one another in order to stir up love and good works.

Ready, Set, Go!

You know, sometimes the people who do the most in our lives are the most ignored. Do you ever feel unappreciated? Do you ever get tired of cleaning your room, doing homework, and brushing your teeth? Do you ever get tired of just being good? That hardly ever gets noticed, does it? *(Pause.)*

Sometimes it seems that people only notice when we do something bad, or something they don't like. "Don't kick the table." "Chew with your mouth closed." "Why did you do *that?*"

Rarely do we hear: "Look, you ate your broccoli and helped your brother get to the table!" "Look, you kept yourself clean today!" "You worked hard today, even though you were tired! Thank you!" *(Wait for groans, nods, a few comments.)*

Well, we often forget to appreciate what our pastor does too. Our pastor has done a lot for us! *(Give examples, such as visited you at the hospital and so on.)* Pastor _____ spends the week writing our sermon, often misses meals, stays up late ministering to others, and takes long road trips to visit the sick and those in need. Yet, I rarely notice. I never really say thank you.

Did you know this is Clergy Appreciation Week? *(Pause.)* Isn't it sad that someone has to remind us to say thank you? *(Pause.)* I wouldn't even have thought about it this week if it hadn't been on the calendar. Fortunately, we have many people in our church who remembered, and that reminded me too! So we brought a little something to show that we love you, Pastor _____. We appreciate how you _____. *(If the children are talkative, ask them to add to the compliments. What means a lot to them? While they answer, give the baked goods/gifts to the appointed child to deliver.)*

Well, next time we're feeling tired and unappreciated, maybe we can turn that around. Maybe we fix that by doing something for someone else—our pastor, parents, friends— even our brothers and sisters. Then we all will feel good. Imagine that!

Let's pray. *(Ask a child to pray or use the following.)* Father, we know you see the hard work and sweet heart of our pastor. Please, Father, bless our pastor as he (she) does quiet deeds, big and small. Please bless our pastor's family, and thank you for the sweetness they add to our church. We know that they too serve in untold ways. And for all those who never hear it, who make coffee, prepare lessons, bake treats, turn on the heat, and pay the bills, bless them, Lord. We need them and appreciate the home they make here for all of us. Amen.

Lights out!

A Thanksgiving Gratitude Check

The Point of It All

We have *much* to be grateful for. But am I?

Objects

Flashlight
Candles
Matches
Gratitude list (see below)

To Dos

Pray and make a gratitude list. Do you have a home? Food in the fridge? Lights? Is your family safe? Is your country free? Do you have love to give? Can you see to read this? To drive yourself where you want to go?

Close your eyes tight and imagine you are blind and will never see again. You must get dressed for church, fix your hair, help others get ready, fix breakfast, study this lesson, and so on. Will you drive to church today? Will you fix lunch? What is the one thing you want now? Pray for it: "God, please let me see the beauty of your world and those I love." Now open your eyes. *(If you have time, walk around blindfolded for a while. You'll never forget it and will have the bruises to prove it! Kids of all ages love this exercise. You can save it for an impromptu Sunday school class [sick teacher day] or for a vacation Bible school activity.)*

Verses to Pray On

Psalm 33:12

Blessed is the nation whose God is the LORD,
And the people whom He has chosen as His own inheritance.

Psalm 144:15

Happy are the people whose God is the LORD!

Ready, Set, Go!

Good to see you! I have an idea. Close your eyes and pretend you're blind. Think as I'm talking. Think about what you had to do this morning before you got to where you are right now. Would it be harder if you were blind? *(Pause for answers.)* OK, open your eyes.

Now, have you ever had your electricity go out? Was that a problem? *(Pause.)* What do you want more than anything when the power goes off? *(Pause.)* The house is dark. You shouldn't open the fridge. The ice cream melts! You have no TV and no air conditioning or heat. That's tough, isn't it? And usually when the power goes off, it is because the weather is bad, so you can't even play outside.

Aren't you happy when the lights come back on? Me too!

This morning when you got out of bed, were you grateful for lights to turn on? For a radio and its music? Did you jump out of bed and shout, "Hooray! I can see!"?

The truth is, I didn't either!

We have many blessings, but we take most of them for granted. We can see, the TV works, we have a God who loves us, parents, friends, and family. So, I made a gratitude list this morning—a list of what I'm thankful for. I'll try to keep it someplace special for when things go wrong. Sometimes I need to remember how many blessings I have. They *always* outweigh the troubles. *Always.*

I don't think I'll ever be happy about the bad things in life, but it does help to see the good. What a loving Father we have. Our blessings are proof of how much he cares.

Let's pray. *(Ask a child to pray or use the following.)* Father, you give us so much. I forget sometimes and take it all for granted. But today I want to say thank you. Thank you, Father, for everything. For each other. For your love. Amen.

Birthday Gifts for Jesus

The Point of It All

Christmas is about giving gifts—gifts of love, nurture, and caring; gifts from us, to others, for Jesus.

Objects

Wrapped boxes or cards; anything representing a lot of gifts

If you or your church normally buys gifts for the kids, this is a great time to pass them out.

A list like Santa's (see below)

Use a large basket to carry all of the above. Tuck some candy canes or loose greens in and add a bow. All will add to the festivity and excitement.

To Dos

Prepare the above objects.

To make "Santa's" list, tape several pieces of paper together one under the other.

Make a gift list for yourself. What will you give to Christ, or give in his name to others, during the coming year? Will you visit a lonely neighbor? Run errands for an older person? Commit to call a certain someone once a week or write them once a month, no matter what the outcome? Now, write the items on your list on "Santa's" list, roll it, and tie with a pretty bow.

Verses to Pray On

John 15:11–13

These things I have spoken to you, that My joy may remain in you, and that your joy may be full. This is My commandment, that you love one another as I have loved you. Greater love has no one than this, than to lay down one's life for his friends.

Acts 3:6

Then Peter said, "Silver and gold I do not have, but what I do have I give you: In the name of Jesus Christ of Nazareth, rise up and walk."

Ready, Set, Go!

Good to see you! Look at what I have today. *(Waggle the gifts in front of them as a tease, like you're going to give the gifts to them. Then pull the gifts back.)*

Don't you love gifts? Bet you can't wait to open yours, can you? Me either! But look at all the stuff I bought for the people I love. *(Waggle gifts at them again!)* I spent hours shopping and making these beautiful gifts—wrapping and planning. I know they will make them happy. That's a nice thing to do at Christmas, isn't it? Aren't you proud of me? Don't you think I'm wonderful?

Oh no! I didn't get you anything! What was I thinking?! Let me look in here *(fish through the obvious abundance)*. Well, I'm sure all you really care about is that my family will get gifts.

(Grin big.) You know I'm teasing you. These gifts *are* for you. But sometimes I wonder if that isn't how Jesus feels. I mean, it's *his* birthday. I never even think to get *him* anything. So this year I'm doing something different. See this big Christmas list I made out? Just like Santa's, isn't it?

(Unroll and display.) I'm committed to giving gifts all throughout this year.

I have people on here to visit, to write, and to help. I'll tell them it's a gift from Jesus. Because he loves them, he wanted them to have this bit of peace, love, or rest. In other words, I'm giving them a gift *from* Jesus, in his name. And that's my gift *to* Jesus.

I love, care for, and share with Jesus by taking care of his kids. What do you think? Can you make a list and check it twice? Give love and hugs—be naughty or nice? It's up to you *(point as you go)*, and you, and you, and me!

Let's pray. *(Ask a child to pray or use the following.)* Happy birthday, Jesus! I'm so glad you were born. You came to care for us, so we could spend all of our time with you. For that gift, we offer you a small token—this year we'll take better care of your kids—kids of all ages. Show us how to serve and love them, even when it's hard, even when we're tired, even when they're cranky. This year let my gift to you be given day after day. Amen.

Santa Claus

The Point of It All

Santa Claus is fun. But he is like artificial sweetener versus fudge when compared with Christ. Try to use what the kids know about Santa and his gifts and make the tremendous leap to the giver of love and life.

Objects

None

To Dos

Nothing. You have enough to do this time of year!

Verses to Pray On

Zephaniah 3:17

The LORD your God in your midst, the Mighty One, will save; He will rejoice over you with gladness, He will quiet you with His love, He will rejoice over you with singing.

Isaiah 62:5

And as the bridegroom rejoices over the bride, so shall your God rejoice over you.

Ready, Set, Go!

I love Christmas, don't you? I'm so glad we can share it!

What does Christmas make you think of? (*Pause. Expect a few "Santa Claus!" exclamations.*) Ah, me too. I love celebrating Christ's birthday. And I like Santa too. He gives gifts, shares love, and makes sure each girl and boy knows that someone cares. Santa represents giving and love. What's not to like about that?

Now close your eyes. We're going to imagine someone *wonderful* together. This wonderful being will be right here with us. Ready? Let's gather in a circle and hold hands. OK, now sit down and close your eyes.

Here we go! Imagine a laughing man. *Big!* So big! He's full of love and gifts and giving. He has a very loud laugh. He delights just to see you, to pull you onto his lap and hold you.

He loves *you* and wants to give *you* the very, very best. Even better than you could ever dream of. Do you see him?

Can you hear his laugh? Do you see the sparkle in his eyes? What does he smell like? Is his beard fluffy? Do you hear his deep singing voice? He's so happy to see you, he's singing! His love is so big that it quiets and calms you. With him you are safe and secure—always.

Guess what! He's in the Bible! Yes he is! Listen—keep those eyes closed. Don't make a peep. Zephaniah 3:17 says, "The LORD *your God* in your midst, the Mighty One, will save; He will rejoice over you with gladness, He will quiet you with His love, He will rejoice over you with singing."

Can you see him? He's much bigger than even Santa. He rejoices because of *you*. He's glad because of *you*. His love is so great it can quiet any hurt. In fact, God loves you *sooo* much, he sings about it! And we know the gifts he has given—love for you and me, this place to gather in, and the gift of the cross that gives us heaven—together forever.

All of it has been made possible by the birth of one teeny-tiny baby. What an awesome God! And he loves you! You! And you! And me too!

Let's pray. *(Ask a child to pray or use the following.)* Father, Santa is wonderful. We're grateful for the fun he brings. But you, dear Father, you are so much more. And your gifts of love and heaven will last forever. We'll never outgrow them, and we can share them and keep them all at the same time. Thank you for your many gifts—especially the sweet babe in the manger. Amen.

PART 2

Good Stuff in General

Can't You Spare a Mite More?

The Point of It All

God wants us to give the best of what we have. The amount we give isn't as important as how much of *ourselves* we give.

Objects

Lollipops—many more than the number of children in your audience

Two kid accomplices and one adult in the pews

To Dos

Choose a partner in the audience, and give him or her two lollipops.

Pull two kids aside and tell them what you are going to do (see sermon).

Pack yourself with lollipops. If possible, have them hanging out of every pocket. Make the large number clearly visible. Have far more than you would need to treat the kids.

Verses to Pray On

Luke 21:1–4

And He looked up and saw the rich putting their gifts into the treasury, and He saw also a certain poor widow putting in two mites. So he said, "Truly I say to you that this poor widow has put in more than all; for all these out of their abundance have put in offerings for God, but she out of her poverty put in all that she had."

Ready, Set, Go!

(Have so many lollipops on you that you drop one. Unwrap it and quickly pop it in your mouth.) Mmm! This is delicious. Mmm-mmm! *(Look up as if you suddenly notice they are there.)* Oh, I'm sorry. Lollipops are so good— so good that sometimes I forget to share. OK, let's see— there are ten of you. *(Rummage through lollipops. Begin to look skeptical. Doubt you can really spare any.)*

Well, you two are brothers and sisters; maybe you can share. And you're too old. You can do without one, huh? *(Warn these kids ahead of time so you won't hurt their feelings.)* Or maybe you can get one from your mom later. I guess I could share . . . hmmm, eight. I might need the others later. You know how it is—I don't want to cut myself short. I might have an emergency or something. I might need them! Or, uh, yeah. I might meet some *really* hungry kids later today. And besides, I gave you something last week.

(Pass out the eight lollipops. Apologize to the kids who don't get one, but act as if it's not really your fault. Suddenly your "accomplice" stands up in the audience and says, "I have two lollipops.")

Ahh. Wow. *(Turn to the kids and snicker as if the person is an idiot and doesn't have much to share.)* Two lollipops.

Who has more? *(Snicker again at the obvious as the kids point out that you do. Your accomplice walks to the front, smiles at you kindly, and says, "Here guys, I have plenty. Take these.")*

(Indignantly.) Well, I have more. And she only gave two pops. I gave a lot more than that! *(You'll get some curious responses. Now pause, then smile as if you are your sweet self again.)*

Do you know that Jesus says that our friend gave more, because she gave all she had? I barely shared a portion of my plenty! Of course we set this up, but many of us really are that way. We have a pile of lollipops or other things we love, and we don't share.

"What if there's not enough?" we ask.

"What if we run out?" we worry.

"Shouldn't they go and get their own? They should work for those," we think.

We rarely ask, "How can I give all I have?"

Christ told his disciples the story of a widow who gave two mites—we would say pennies today—to the collection plate. He said it counted more than what all the others gave. They may have given five dollars, ten dollars, or even one hundred dollars, but it was only a small bit of what they had—of what *God himself* had blessed them with.

The widow gave everything she had—down to her last penny. Or the last lollipop! How did I make you feel when I didn't share? How do you think God feels when I'm selfish with gifts that he gave me in the first place? How does God feel when I don't share with his other kids?

How can you and I be more willing to give? *(Pause. Smile.)*

Let's pray. *(Ask a child to pray or use the following.)* Father, help us to give our all. Whether it's lollipops, helping around the house, or pennies in the plate, Father, help us to do more for you and your children. Amen.

Bringing Back the Dead

The Point of It All

Only Jesus can make the dead new again.

Object

Dead flower or plant, wrapped "pretty"

To Dos

Let a sickly plant or flower die.

Make the plant or flower pretty with a vase or bow—the "fussier" the better.

Verses to Pray On

Matthew 11:5–6

The blind see and the lame walk; the lepers are cleansed and the deaf hear; the dead are raised up and the poor have the gospel preached to them. And blessed is he who is not offended because of Me.

Ephesians 2:1

And you he made alive, who were dead in trespasses and sins.

Ready, Set, Go!

Don't you all look lovely! Speaking of lovely, look what I've brought. *(Point out the details of your dead plant, only emphasizing the beauty—the bow, the vase, and so on.)* Don't you love it? I spent time this morning making it pretty. Isn't it pretty? And I made it just for you! Here, who wants to hold it?

What? *(Look completely surprised.)* Don't you like the bow? It's my prettiest vase! What do you mean it's dead? Well, yes, I didn't water it for a week or so. OK, I left it out on the kitchen counter for a few *short* weeks without water. But I worked so hard on it this morning! It's just a bit wilted. OK, it's dead. But didn't I fix it up pretty? Here, who wants it? *(If some child actually takes the dead thing, let the child off the hook by complimenting his or her kindness.)*

OK, OK. You know, without Jesus we'd all be dead—spiritually dead—while we live and breathe! We wouldn't have joy. Those who care for us wouldn't be as wonderful as they are. They wouldn't even know how to love us like we need it. Jesus gave us all of that. He taught us, and he sent the Holy Spirit to guide us and keep us company.

Jesus raised Lazarus from the dead, and he came back from the dead himself. But he gives us a life worth living. That's a great blessing, isn't it? I mean, I wouldn't want to look—or feel—like this flower. How about you?

Let's pray. *(Ask a child to pray or use the following.)* Father, you gave us life, and you sent Jesus to give us eternal life. And in between you teach us how to love so that our lives can be beautiful. Thank you for watering our souls every day. All we have to do is ask! Amen.

Are You Plugged In?

The Point of It All

We all need to "plug in" to God's power every day.

Objects

Tape or CD player with no batteries
The cord to the player
Favorite tape or CD of a sweet, soothing song

To Dos

Gather your supplies in an easy-to-use place or container so each pops up in the right order without spoiling the ending.

Get an accomplice who knows where an outlet is and how to use the CD or tape player.

Brief your accomplice on your plans.

Verses to Pray On

John 14:23, 26–27

If anyone loves Me, he will keep My word; and My Father will love him, and We will come to him and make Our home with him. . . . But the Helper, the Holy Spirit, whom the Father will send in My name, He will teach you all things, and bring to your remembrance all things that I said to you. Peace I leave with you, My peace I give to you;

not as the world gives do I give to you. Let not your heart
be troubled, neither let it be afraid.

John 15:1–8

Jesus' teaching on the vine and the branches.

Ready, Set, Go!

I am so excited today! I want to share my favorite song
with you. I have it right here. *(Hold up your cassette or CD.*
Talk about how much you love it, need for them to hear it,
as you put the tape/CD in the player and turn it on. Wait
expectantly, then look confused as nothing happens. Hit sev-
eral buttons. They should be crying out solutions at this
point!)

Batteries, that's right! Batteries. *(Check and discover that*
the chamber is empty.) Ugh! I wish I could sing it for you.
(Sing a few notes as off-key as you can.) There are some
drums right after that—you know, bum, pa pum pum—
and a lady sings. It's really beautiful. I can hear it in my
head right now. *(Pause and look at their faces.)* Not good
enough, huh? OK, we have to solve this. What do we need?
(Pause.)

That's right, the cord. Wait, I brought the cord. It's right
here. I'll plug this end into the player. *(Earnestly work at*
fixing the problem. Look up in exasperation when the player
doesn't start, then hold up the plug end and laugh.) You're
right! I need to plug it in! *(Finally, allow your accomplice*
to plug it into the wall and hit play. Let the music play for a
verse or so.)

OK, thank you. You can turn it off now. I told you the
music was *very* special. Yet I couldn't share it with you
unless I was completely connected to the *right* power, could
I? I could give you *my* words—but you needed to hear the
real music. And I needed the right power source to plug

into so you could hear it. And we all need to plug in—and listen—completely.

It's like that with God. I need to be connected to him, as completely as I can be, so that I can share what I hear, what I know and feel, with others. I see his beauty, his power and love—and then others can too!

So, how do we plug in? *(Pause.)* That's right. Gather with friends in church, ask questions, read our Bibles, pray, and pray with others. We can ask God to be with us, and he will come into our hearts—no batteries or cord needed!

Jesus promised, "If anyone loves Me, he will keep My word; and My Father will love him, and We will come to him and make Our home with him." And that sweet music lasts longer than a lifetime.

Let's pray. *(Ask a child to pray or use the following.)* Father, you offer us the most loving home of all. When we feel like we can handle life "all by ourselves," help us to come to you first. And when we're lonely or hurting, help us to reach out and remember that you never leave us. Remind us to plug in that cord—to pray or call a friend who will remind us of your love and care. Amen.

A Road Map for Life

The Point of It All

God's way and God's Word will take us where we want to be.

Objects

Road map
Bible

Small toy bus to run over the map

To Dos

Rest, journal, have a cup of tea or coffee, and relax.

Think about how God's journey has turned out well in your life. Try to remember a few detours you took that left you lost. Can you share them with the kids or with a friend who needs to hear?

Verse to Pray On

Psalm 119:105

Your word is a lamp to my feet, and a light to my path.

Ready, Set, Go!

Welcome! Good to see you! Do you know what this is? *(Hold up map.)* That's right! Why do people use maps? *(Pause.)*

Today we're going to pretend that we are going to your favorite park. Close your eyes for a second and really see it. Got it? OK. Now we're all going together as a group. We have a bright, new bus and a friendly driver. He pulls up, and one by one, we all get on the bus. We sit down and get quiet, and the bus driver hollers happily, "Let's go!"

We pull to the edge of the church lot, and the bus driver speaks more softly this time. "Hmm," he says, "I wonder which way I should turn? Right looks good. Hey, left looks good too! Oh well! I'll just pick one!"

He flips a coin and decides to turn left. You're pretty sure the park is right.

How happy are we? *(Pause.)* I agree. I don't want to be on a bus with a driver who doesn't know where he is going.

71

If he doesn't know the way, we'll never get where we need to go. So then what does he need? *(Pause.)* That's right! A road map to show him the way.

It's the same for us. Sometimes we need help in our decisions. God has given us a road map—the Bible. It's made up of God's words and tells us which way to turn if we want to be safe and happy in life. But we need to stop, get out the map, and look at the directions he's given us.

God is our Father. He knows the way, and he loves us. He doesn't want us to get lost or hurt. He wants us to come home safe and have a good time. But if we get lost on the way, feel unsure or afraid, we can just open that map—our Bible—and check it out. We can find the right road again, the road to a life of love and freedom with Christ and our Father. And that road will take us to the best park we could ever imagine—heaven!

Let's pray. *(Ask a child to pray or use the following.)* Father, help us to remember that you didn't give us your words to spoil our journey, but to take us on the most beautiful ride ever. You know the best way and want the best for us, because we are your kids, and you love us very, very much. Thanks for that. It is *truly* a blessing. Amen.

Cleaning out Closets

The Point of It All

If we clean the clutter out of our minds, we can really *be* with God in prayer.

Objects

Large garbage bag filled with miscellaneous things you might find on a closet floor: one sock, a childhood game, an old shoe, a crumpled piece of paper, an out-dated outfit. Try to make it bulky and funny. You can even have a skeleton for your closet! Pad the bottom of the bag with crumpled newspapers to give it bulk.

Make sure to add a Bible—something important that gets lost in the clutter.

To Dos

Practice pulling stuff out of the bag. You want to make it look cumbersome but also be able to clean up in time to leave the "stage."

Spend time in prayer, and practice "uncluttering" your mind. You might share some of your life experiences with the kids. Better yet, share your failures and what you're doing about them. We all want to improve and be even closer to God. Kids need to know that they're not alone in their Christian journey.

Verse to Pray On

Matthew 6:6

But you, when you pray, go into your room [KJV, "closet"], and when you have shut your door, pray to your Father who is in the secret place; and your Father who sees in secret will reward you openly.

Ready, Set, Go!

Do you have a closet? *(Pause.)* Closets seem to gather stuff, and sometimes we have to clean them out, don't we? *(Pause.)* Well, I have to clean out my closets pretty often. *(Talk about cleaning out your child's closet or fill in with a tale from your own life.)* Cleaning out a closet can be quite a job.

We usually make three piles of the stuff we take out: things to move to another closet *(smile big and wink)*, stuff to give away, and stuff to toss out. *(As you're talking, pull stuff from the bag. Remember to be funny. As you pull each piece out, look surprised.)*

What a mess, huh? I find a lot of stuff I don't expect to find—every time! *(Pull out the skeleton or something silly.)* But when I'm done, I always have more room. Better still, I can find what I need—like my favorite jeans. *(Or one last silly thing—like a rubber ducky!)*

Did you know that there's a closet in the Bible? *(Pull out the last thing—your Bible.)* Oh no, let's hope our Bible's not in the closet! Anyway, there *is* a closet in the Bible. In one verse, Jesus says that when you pray, go into your closet, shut your door, and pray. He means that we should pray in a quiet, secret, uncluttered place. See? If that room were all cluttered, there wouldn't be room to pray.

Sometimes we get all cluttered inside—worrying, dreaming, thinking of what we want to do next. We need to clean out that stuff too. We can't fit God in a cluttered mind any more than we can fit into a cluttered closet—or a cluttered bedroom. *(Laugh and smile.)*

Maybe we can start our prayer *with* a prayer—like this: "God, please help me clean out my worries and focus on you. Help me to see only you, dream only of you when I pray today." Then we can really hear the prayers we say and know what God wants us to learn from them. And things will be less likely to bonk us on the head.

Let's pray. *(Ask a child to pray or use the following.)* Father, you know how hard it can be to clear our minds. We live in a busy world with much to think about. Help us to see prayer as the rest that it is. Help us to hold on to you, to see you. Please clear out the clutter so we can truly be with you—because that is where we want to be. Amen.

Are You Fruity?

The Point of It All

What fruit do we produce? Can we really see it for what it is?

Objects

Bright and beautiful apple or one for each child

Nasty, bruised, shriveled apple. If no old-timers are growing moldy in your fridge, try the "older" fruit section in your supermarket. Let your kids play catch with the apple a few days before you need it.

Pretty bag or cookie box in which to pack the nasty apple

To Dos

Take a steamy shower or a bubble bath—whatever opens your mind to God's direction.

Have a cup of hot chocolate with whipped topping or a crisp apple.

Watch the sun rise or set with your Bible in hand. (You deserve it! You, my friend, are a child of the King.)

Verses to Pray On

Galatians 5:22–26

The fruit of the Spirit is love, joy, peace, longsuffering, kindness, goodness, faithfulness, gentleness, self-control. Against such there is no law. And those who are Christ's have crucified the flesh with its passions and desires. If we live in the Spirit, let us also walk in the Spirit. Let us not become conceited, provoking one another, envying one another.

Hebrews 12:11–16

Now, no chastening seems to be joyful for the present, but painful: nevertheless, afterward it yields the peaceable fruit of righteousness to those who have been trained by it. Therefore strengthen the hands which hang down, and the feeble knees, and make straight paths for your feet, so that what is lame may not be dislocated, but rather be healed. Pursue peace with all people, and holiness, without which no one will see the Lord: looking carefully lest anyone fall short of the grace of God; lest any root of bitterness springing up cause trouble, and by this many become defiled; lest there be any fornicator or profane person like Esau, who for one morsel of food sold his birthright.

Ready, Set, Go!

Every Sunday morning I get up, stretch, and smile. I truly look forward to this time with you! Well, today I have something wonderful to give you. Who wants one? *(Wave your fruit-filled container. Pause for answers and keep your moldy fruit in the container.)*

Good, good. Because I have much to share with you this morning—apples! *(Pull out the moldy oldie and offer it to the kids. Look confused at their reaction.)* What? It is *too* an apple! I worked hard for this apple. And you deserve it. Here. Take a bite. *(No matter how hard they fight you, just smile and shake your head. Refuse to admit that this is a nasty apple.)*

OK. Prove it. *(Pause. Finally, admit that you must agree. Act as if you see the moldy oldie for the first time.)* Jumping jelly donuts! You're right! My goodness, I almost gave that to you. It most certainly would have made you sick if you had believed it was "good fruit." *(Shake your head at your own silliness.)*

Did you know that Jesus spoke about fruit a lot? He wanted us to have good fruit—not to eat, but to grow. The apostle Paul wrote this to the churches of Galatia: "The fruit of the Spirit is love, joy, peace, longsuffering, kindness, goodness, faithfulness, gentleness, self-control. Against such there is no law" (Galatians 5:22–23). He meant that if we follow the Holy Spirit, we will have love, joy, peace, and patience, and we will be kind, good, faithful, and gentle. We will also learn self-control. God can give it all—and it will show like bountiful apples on a tree. *(Pull out your apple or basket of apples now. If a basket, allow a child to pass them out.)*

The point? Our fruit can go bad if we're not paying attention. We need to stay close to God so he can keep us blooming with his many blessings. Which do you want? This *(thrust the moldy fruit back among them)* or this *(take a deep whiff of the beautiful apple)*? You get to choose!

Let's pray. *(Ask a child to pray or use the following.)* Father, help me to stop and smell the fruit. Do I show love and patience, or do I need to come back to you for a pruning? Help me to see what you want for me. Amen.

Wonderful, Counselor, Mighty God, Prince of Peace

The Point of It All

Jesus fulfills many roles for us—friend, counselor, father, protector, and many more. Likewise, we fulfill many roles for others he loves—mother, father, wife, husband, brother, sister, son, daughter, child, friend, and so on.

Objects

Picture from a magazine or a children's book about family. It needs to picture a variety of family members—for example: father, brother, sister, grandparents. It must be visible from a distance—funny, bright pictures work best.

Bible

To Dos

Pray about the many roles you fulfill: your parents' child, your child's parent, protector, teacher, sibling, and so on. Look at how these roles change over the years but still need to involve honor, love, and respect.

Pray about the roles you have in relationship to our Father and to Christ. Are you his servant, friend, and growing child? Is he your counselor? Protector? How has your relationship changed over the years?

Read and place a bookmark at Isaiah 9:6. Be prepared to quote it in your lesson.

Verse to Pray On

Isaiah 9:6

For unto us a Child is born, unto us a Son is given;
and the government will be upon His shoulder.
And His name will be called Wonderful, Counselor,
Mighty God, Everlasting Father, Prince of Peace.

Ready, Set, Go!

Hey, did you know that we're brothers and sisters—in Christ? In fact, we are called by many names. For example *(fill in the names to match you),* I'm Michael and Matthew's mom. They call me Mom. My husband calls me Annette or sometimes . . . honey! *(Pause before saying "honey." The audience will laugh as they fill in the blank for you.)*

My mom's name is Betty, but I never call her that. I call her Mom. And I never called my dad Stan; I called him Daddy. Grandpa was Grandpa—never, ever Leo, although that's what he was to Grandma, his "Shug" *(short for "Sugar," but you'll be filling in your own blanks).*

In other words, you might be a sister, a son, a brother, a friend at home. At school you're a student, a classmate, or a teammate. You are each of these things to each of these people. And you mean different things to each of these friends and fellow students, even those you don't know that well and just pass in the halls.

Isaiah 9:6 reads, "For unto us a Child is born, unto us a Son is given; and the government will be upon His shoulder. And His name will be called Wonderful, Counselor, Mighty God, Everlasting Father, Prince of Peace." Each of these names of Jesus—Wonderful, Counselor, Mighty God, Everlasting Father, Prince of Peace—describes Jesus and the many things he is to us. *(Talk about what you found when praying. How has Jesus filled these roles for you?)*

When do you need Jesus? *(Pause for some beautiful, thought-provoking answers.)* And when does Jesus need you? *(Pause.)* That's right. He needs you to help him take care of his other kids—young and old. Moms and dads, brothers and sisters, teammates, and even those we just pass in the hallway. A smile can be a powerful thing, especially on a hard or lonely day.

Jesus, the Prince of Peace, comforts me when I feel sad. Sometimes he'll even send another of his kids to help. My children bring a hug, or ask if I'm OK. My husband does the dishes, or makes a simple dinner.

And sometimes, I'm blessed to be the one God sends to help—to hug my kids after a hard day, or to scratch my husband's back, or pack a quick snack to boost his spirit at work.

Jesus loves his kids. And, young and old, we *are* Jesus' kids. God's kids. We are well loved. We are blessed to be sons and daughters of the *true King!*

Let's pray. *(Ask a child to pray or use the following.)* Father, help us to remember that you are all things to all of us. When we need a friend, you are there. When we are worried, you are there. Even until the end of time, you are there waiting with open arms. Amen.

Spiders in My Hair

The Point of It All

We all have fears that magnify reality. What can I do the next time fear attacks?

Objects

Flashlight

Cutout of a moth or bat taped to a flashlight face (over the light) with clear tape

Rubber spider or insect

A few bits of nature from outside—a rock, a pretty leaf, or flowered branches from a blooming tree in spring

To Dos

Practice flying your flashlight "bat" around the room.

Arrange to have the lights turned down to near darkness after the kids are safely settled. Arrange to have the lights raised at your prompt.

Relax. Reflect on your own fears (sickness, debt, loneliness, a difficult coworker, learning something new). Sometimes we cover up fears just by avoiding a task or thought. The more we realize we all have irrational fears, the more we can help God's other kids with theirs—and ask God to heal our own.

Verses to Pray On

2 Timothy 1:3–7

Without ceasing I remember you in my prayers night and day, greatly desiring to see you, being mindful of your tears, that I may be filled with joy, when I call to remembrance the genuine faith that is in you, which dwelt first in your grandmother Lois and your mother Eunice, and I am persuaded is in you also. Therefore I remind you to stir up the gift of God which is in you through the laying on of my hands. For God has not given us a spirit of fear, but of power and of love and of a sound mind.

2 Timothy 1:14

*That good thing which was committed to you,
keep by the Holy Spirit who dwells in you.*

Ready, Set, Go!

I love how I can count on you to be here with me. It
would feel awful to be alone up here. *(The lights go out—
but in a manner that won't frighten the little ones. If you
have a "sensitive" audience, assure some of the timid ones
ahead of time, or make it less dramatic, and just dim the
lights.)*

Oh my! Well, luckily, I have a flashlight with me. And
you're here! We'll be OK until they get that fixed. *(Flash
your light around. Finally, hit a blank wall so the bat appears
to fly. Quick swipes of your flashlight will make the bat look* ✎
like it is swooping.) Wow! What was that? *(Swipe again and
again. Make funny faces. Try to hide behind one of the smaller
children.)*

Is that a bat? Uh, oh! *(Laugh and look at the end of your
flashlight.)* Silly me! It's only a bit of paper. See? *(Quickly
pull it off. Cue the lights to come back on.)*

You know, I have to admit, that's happened to me before.
I thought a small shadow was something big and scary.
One night I *(use "a friend of mine" or change to a similar
story of your own)* was walking in the dark and a moth in
a streetlamp looked like a gigantic bat flying around my
head! I ducked *(duck)* and spun around quickly to find a
harmless little moth. I felt so silly!

Still, it took me a few minutes and a few prayers to settle down. My heart was pounding!

It was only a moth. But the darkness—and my fear—
made it look like it would bite my head off. Or get tangled
in my hair. Yikes! *(Make a face complete with silly eyes and
lean toward your audience.)*

82

Did you ever get a spider in your hair? *(Flip your rubber spider at an older kid.)* That can *really* make you dance around! *(Pantomime flicking a spider from your hair wildly. Stop, and smile soothingly again.)* Each time something like that happens and I "freak out," I promise that I'll never do *that* again. I'll pray instead!

I know fear makes moths into bats—and turns the sweet secrets of night into fear and fright. But in the moment, I forget sometimes. Some things *are* scary. But if I'm busy being afraid all the time, I miss the beauty of God's world. The song of the crickets. The beauty of a streetlight. The absolute miracle of an undisturbed spider web covered with diamonds of dew just before the sun rises. *(Show the nature bits from your yard, and talk about them. Let the children hold them.)*

I may not be calm every time something frightens me. I am sure I will still be afraid sometimes. After all, God gave me a healthy sense of fear to keep me from being hurt. That way I know enough to check things out. For instance, I can ask, Is it really a large bat? Do I need to run? Or should I just turn around and say a prayer to settle my heart and then take a few breaths and relax? *(Shake out your arms.)* Try this: SHHHSHHH *(breath out loudly).* You do it: SHHHSHHH. Good. Now, shake your arms. Make them wiggly. Now let's say a little prayer and see if we don't feel better.

(Ask a child to pray or use the following.) Father, you gave us fear to keep us safe. Help us to slow down, check things out, and pray for a solution. If we're afraid of a mere moth, help us to settle down and enjoy the beautiful day you've made. Amen.

Birds' Nest Down

The Point of It All

Tragedy comes to everybody. We don't earn or deserve it—it's just a consequence of living.

Objects

Bird's nest or picture of one

Bits of string, pine needles, or leaves—anything a bird would weave into a nest

Clump of dirt, clay, or mud

Large glass container in which to display bird nest "parts"

To Dos

Watch birds. Tour your yard and try to find part of a bird's nest or download a picture of one from the Internet. They truly are a wonder of work, love, and nurture.

Think about an injustice you saw or experienced—either in nature or in your life.

Verses to Pray On

Psalm 34:19–20 NIV

A righteous man may have many troubles, but the LORD delivers him from them all; he protects all his bones, not one of them will be broken.

Ready, Set, Go!

Hi, guys! It's good to see you again! We're kind of like birds, aren't we? We return to this safe, cozy nest again and again. Do you ever watch birds? *(Pause.)* I do. I love birds. They're so smart!

(Describe a story you've witnessed, or use this story and start with "A friend of mine.") We have birds' nests hidden all over our yard. My family loves to watch the mama birds care for their babies. We love to watch the papa birds bring wiggly worms and crunchy bugs. Mmm! *(Grin and wiggle your eyes and say, "Oh, gross!")* I love how hard they work as a family. It takes a lot of searching to find food for all those hungry beaks.

I'm always stunned by birds' dedication to each other. And their nests! All the pieces *(show your pieces)* are collected one at a time and are woven neatly and completely into the others to make a nest for their babies.

But every once in a while, after a big, windy storm, I find one of those carefully constructed nests on the ground. The family gone. Cracked, never-to-be hatched eggs nearby. I think, *What a waste! How sad! Those birds didn't do anything but work hard and take care of each other. What did they do to deserve this? Is God punishing them?* What do you think? *(Pause.)*

Did you know that even the good guys in the Bible had trouble? Even Moses? Even Noah? Can you imagine how hard it was for Noah to live in that ark for so long? To lose all his neighbors and friends? And he was the lucky one! Life can be hard—and no one *deserves* that. Jesus *never* sinned—and look what he went through.

The Bible says we're going to have many problems. Many. But God will be there to help us, to comfort us, to send friends and family to talk about it. Sometimes he'll even send a miracle to help us out. And always, no matter what, God promises us a happy ending—heaven, where we'll all be together. No tears. No sadness. None. The ultimate nest to fly home to—and Jesus has promised to get it ready. Just for you and me!

Let's pray. *(Ask a child to pray or use the following.)* Father, bad things do happen—to all of us. But you are there to comfort us. And when we need arms to hold us, you send friends and family—angels in blue jeans and sneakers—to share your love. Thank you, Father, for all you do! Amen.

Broken Toys

The Point of It All

Jesus never throws away the broken or the injured. In fact, he pulls us closer.

Objects

A few broken toys—the nicer the better (it's more of a loss to break a new or "cool" toy than a rusty, old one)

Ace bandage or crutch—anything that denotes a physical break in your body

To Dos

Wrap your forearm in a bulky Ace bandage—maybe with a flat board beneath it. Practice limping crazily to add to your wounded appearance.

Relax and reflect on the ways people can be broken. Has God ever healed you or someone you care about? Even if you can't share the miracle, having it on your heart can bring a lot to the service.

Verse to Pray On

Psalm 147:3

He heals the brokenhearted and binds up their wounds.

Ready, Set, Go!

(Limp heavily to stage. Hold your arm and moan. Move suddenly and grab your neck. If any of the children look "overly worried," wink and smile at them quickly, but then continue to limp.) Good morning! Well, at least I *wish* it was. Look at my arm, my head, my neck! Oh my, am I ever hurting! I fell out of the wrong side of the bed this morning. Now what will I do? *(Pause. Grin big.)*

You know, I'm teasing you a bit, but I want to show you something. *(Pull out your toys one by one.)* Look at these. Have you ever broken something you care about? You were just going along, playing, having fun, and bam! Crack! Boom! Broken!

Stinks, doesn't it? Or you decided to try something you were told not to do—we all do that sometimes *(grimace in sympathy)*—and bam! Crack! Boom! Broken!

Then you try to fix it. But have you ever tried to fix a badly broken toy—a hopeless one with cracked wheels and shattered plastic? How does it work afterward? *(Try to put a wheel back on. Let it wobble.)*

I know. Sometimes it's a mess, isn't it? Sometimes when I break a favorite thing, I just stuff it away somewhere. I hope *somebody* can fix it. Soon I just forget about it or, finally, throw it away.

You know, sometimes people get broken too. No, not like this. *(Point to your fake injuries.)* Doctors fix that. Bigger breaks—like their heart. Or they wander away from church and family, and they change—almost as if they *are* broken. But God never lets go. He never throws us away or stuffs us in a closet. He loves us and keeps his hand on us—even when we seem hopelessly broken. He heals us or searches for us. He never forgets. And he never gives up—because God can heal anything. Absolutely anything. What a blessing! *(Do a little flourish with your broken arm or, if standing, a mini dance step with your broken feet.)*

Let's pray. *(Ask a child to pray or use the following.)* Father, thank you that you never toss us away or forget about us. We are grateful that you have the power and the love to heal us. When we're hurting or just off track, please heal us. Make us good as new—for only you can do that. Amen.

Name It! Claim It!

The Point of It All

Jesus lives up to his many names, and he knows our names.

Objects

Book of baby names
Your own baby picture
Bible

To Dos

Look up the names of the kids you minister to or the meaning of your pastor's name and a few others in your church. Find out (if you don't know) why your name was chosen and what it means. What does it mean to you? If easier, you can talk about your dog's name.

Pray about the importance of knowing God's name and calling out for him in prayer. How has God helped you? Did you have to do more than merely ask?

Verses to Pray On

Proverbs 18:10

The name of the LORD is a strong tower;
The righteous run to it and are safe.

Proverbs 22:1

A good name is to be chosen rather than great riches.

Isaiah 9:6

For unto us a Child is born, unto us a Son is given;
and the government will be upon His shoulder.
And His name will be called Wonderful, Counselor,
Mighty God, Everlasting Father, Prince of Peace.

Zechariah 13:9

They will call on My name.

Matthew 6:9

Hallowed be Your name.

Revelation 2:13

You hold fast to My name.

Ready, Set, Go!

Good morning, Jolly Jake! Sally Sue! The Bob-ster! Janey! Scooter! *(Look pointedly at each child, pat a few on the arm as you "mistakenly" name them. Call them each by silly names.)* Doesn't Pastor Smiley look wonderful today? *(Again, act as if you got his name correct.)* What? Those aren't your names? I know, but so what? *(Pause for complaints.)*

That's right. Names are very important! If I couldn't think of my son's name, I couldn't even warn him of a speeding car or an angry dog! I couldn't call my husband to dinner. My son couldn't get my attention to ask for a glass of water at night.

But names mean even more than that. Let me show you something. This is what I looked like as a baby. *(Show picture.)* And my mom named me _____ because _____. See this book of baby names? It shows the meaning of nearly every name there is. For example, . . . *(Explain some of those you looked up. Read the meanings of the names and discuss how carefully parents consider selecting just the right name for their baby. Then read Isaiah 9:6.)*

Each of Jesus' names is important: Wonderful, Counselor, Mighty God, Everlasting Father, Prince of Peace. I bet you like it better when I call you by your true names, don't you? *(Name and point to a few.)* I like that better too. I like who you are. I love that when I think of your names, I think of sweet friends. I love that when I think of Pastor _____, I think of caring leadership. And I am grateful that when I think of Jesus, I know he's the Prince of Peace, Mighty God, Everlasting Father, and too many wonderful things to even say in a day. And he is!

Let's pray. *(Ask a child to pray or use the following.)* Father God, Friend, Comforter, and Counselor, thank you for living up to your many names. And thank you for each of

these lovely children who surround me. We are grateful
that *you* care enough to know our names too. Amen.

What Comforts You?

The Point of It All

Paul said God comforts us "in all our tribulation" so that
we can comfort others in their own tribulations.

Objects

Bag full of comfort items—Bible, telephone, snuggle
blanket, doll or stuffed animal, bag of unpopped popcorn, music tape or CD, packet of hot chocolate—
include what truly comforts you and those you love

Notebook and pen

To Dos

Rest and pray about 2 Corinthians 1:2–5. What truly
comforts you? What trouble (even if too private to
share) has God comforted you through? How have
you been able to use a horrible experience to comfort
and counsel another later?

How about when you were a child? Were you ever
scorned? Teased? Hated, even? These are great things
to journal about. Christ has "been there" and knows
how to help. Make sure the kids know that by the time
you're through.

Verses to Pray On

2 Corinthians 1:2–5

*Grace to you and peace from God our Father and the Lord
Jesus Christ. Blessed be the God and Father of our Lord
Jesus Christ, the Father of mercies and God of all comfort, who comforts us in all our tribulation, that we may
be able to comfort those who are in any trouble, with the
comfort with which we ourselves are comforted by God.
For as the sufferings of Christ abound in us, so our conso-
lation also abounds through Christ.*

Ready, Set, Go!

Oh, it is so comforting to know you'll be here each week!
*(Smile and carefully dig into your bag/basket. Pull out a snug-
gle bunny or child's blanket.)* Look what I brought to show
you. Umm! I love these "snugglies." They used to make me
feel *so good* when I was little.

Today I still love *(continue to pull from the bag and name
your items)* a cup of hot chocolate or a nice bowl of crunchy
popcorn when I'm really sad. I play some music, hug my
kids *(or "dog" or "pillow")*, or call a friend who cares. *(Leave
the Bible for last.)* Sometimes I read my Bible and write
about how I feel. *(Pull out a notebook and pen.)* What do
you do when you're really upset? *(Pause.)* Me too! It helps,
doesn't it?

You know what? God wants to help comfort us. And then
he wants us to share that comfort with others we love.
Maybe they need a hug. Maybe our grandma needs a short
letter or a phone call. Maybe Dad would just like you to sit
and watch a ballgame with him—even if he doesn't want
to talk.

We all need somebody who cares—really, really cares.
And even if it's a day when it *feels* like nobody cares, and

even if it is one of those hurting days, you *know* God is there. He cares. A lot! So he has sent us many tools to use— Jesus to love, live, and die for us, others to give us hugs, and the Bible to look up what God says about it all.

Then, when the tough stuff is all over and we're back to skipping rope, we can help others, because we'll be a bit stronger. And that is being a tool of God too!

Let's pray. *(Ask a child to pray or use the following.)* Father, I know you are ready to comfort us when we hurt. Help us to remember to turn to you and your Bible so that we may heal. Help us to reach out and hug others so they may feel better too. Amen.

A Peek at Heaven

The Point of It All

If we could get a peek at heaven, how hard would we try to get there? Our lives can be a peek at heaven, a peek at what Jesus' love can do.

Objects

Large bag that you can't see through
Something that makes a noise at the push of a button

To Dos

Pray and ask God to show you a "peek of heaven" in a few of the kids you minister to—or in several key people in your congregation. You'll use what you find in the sermon.

Practice making your "something wonderful" sound off inside the bag.

Verses to Pray On

John 14:1–2

Let not your heart be troubled; you believe in God, believe also in Me. In My Father's house are many mansions; if it were not so, I would have told you. I go to prepare a place for you.

Ready, Set, Go!

(Sit down with the big bag at your side. Appear very happy, as if you have a secret. Make your noisemaker "sound off" a time or two, but make your movement "secret." Continue to sound off as you teach.)

Good morning! Are you having a great morning? I am! *(Squeeze bag and smile. Nod like they should know what you're enjoying.)*

You know, I was thinking. What if . . . what if you could get a peek at heaven? *(Buzz, buzz.)* Just a peek? Maybe spend a few minutes there?

Would you *(buzz)* ever think of anything else? Would you do anything to get *(buzz)* there? Would you at least stop and ask directions?

Well, what if you met someone who was like a bit of heaven? Someone as peaceful or as joyous as heaven? Would you want to be like that person? Would you want to know how that person *(buzz)* got that way? *(Buzz, buzz.)*

(By now, hopefully they've stopped paying attention to you. They want to know only what is in the bag. Make it buzz loudly. Then pull the toy/gadget out of the bag.)

Ahh, it's been hard to think of anything but this toy, hasn't it? You want it, don't you? You want it because it makes me happy and looks like fun! It's hard to think about anything else, isn't it?

(Put "heaven" back in the bag. Move the bag behind you— away from the kids. Give them a second or two to resettle and comment.)

I have another secret: You can be just like heaven! You can be someone other people want to be. You can be that bit of heaven—love, kindness, peace, joy.

When we get to know God and let him really become a part of us—when we share God's work, talk to him, and spend time with his people—we become *that* bit of heaven. We easily share love, kindness, and happiness.

And then others want what we have. And then they'll ask, "Hey, what is that special something you have?" And you can show them what you have hidden, not in a bag, not just a silly toy, but that you have Christ in your heart. And you want to share him. Neat, huh?

Let's pray. *(Ask a child to pray or use the following.)* Father, you have given me so many gifts; help me to share them with others so that we may all make it to your golden gates. Amen.

Disney World in a Baggie

The Point of It All

Not all prayers are answered, but we need to show our faith that God hears our prayers and knows what is best for us all.

Objects

Baggies filled with travel items (snacks, tissues, anything you might use at Disney World)
Umbrellas
Raincoats or an extra set of clothing

To Dos

Pray about something you need—big or small. Do you have faith that God will provide (after our "footwork" is finished, of course), or will you soon get impatient and lose faith?

Verse to Pray On

2 Corinthians 5:7

We walk by faith, not by sight.

Ready, Set, Go!

I have a friend who took her daughters to Disney World when they were ages ten and thirteen. They spent months planning and saving for the big trip. But when they arrived in their hotel, it was rainy. My friend was very worried. She and her husband didn't want to disappoint their girls. They listened to the weather forecast on TV and heard the worst. An entire day of rain—the one day they had to spend touring the park!

Well, my friend is not a silly person, but she just couldn't bear what her girls would feel the next day—soaked and sad! So she decided to pray: "Lord, please, *if it is your will,* let the day be nice and filled with sunshine. We have come so far for this trip. The girls are so excited! Help us have a great day, Father. Amen."

Well, some people might call that a silly prayer. *(Pause.)* I know! But it wasn't. That rainy day turned into a *beautiful* day filled with sunshine. They had a great day, just like my friend had prayed for. Suddenly, though, my friend felt bad. She looked in her bag. She had prepared for rain. *(Pull out items as you talk.)* Umbrellas, extra clothes for the girls, everything packed neatly in rainproof bags. *What must God think of me?* she thought with a laugh. *I asked, I prayed, but I never believed he would care. I never believed he would help.*

You know, I have to admit, sometimes I've prayed for things and I didn't get my way. Sometimes I felt my prayer requests were much more important than a sunny day. I've even watched sick people get sicker and bad things happen. That is always hard for me to understand. In fact, I was told God *always* answers prayers—one of four ways: "Yes," "No," "Maybe later," and "You've got to be kidding!" *(Pause for laughs.)*

When God says no, I still need to have faith that he knows what is best. He knows what we all need. And, in the end, he will make sure the good prospers, because God *is* in control—even if we can't see past the forecast of rain!

Let's pray. *(Ask a child to pray or use the following.)* Father, you are so good to us. Help me to hold on to you when my faith falters. Hold me up and remind me of the sunny days when all I can see is rain. Amen.

Cruisin' with Candy

The Point of It All

Do we listen to our Father?

Objects

Candy bar
Small candy bars to share

To Dos

Hide the small candy bars in a basket.
Think of something you rebel against—bills, food, gossip, speed limits. Is there any nagging, still, small voice that you are ignoring?

Verses to Pray On

Romans 10:17–18

So then faith comes by hearing, and hearing by the word of God. But I say, have they not heard?

Galatians 3:2

This only I want to learn from you: Did you receive the Spirit by the works of the law, or by the hearing of faith?

Ready, Set, Go!

(This really happened to me with my toddler. Change the story to fit your life.) Aren't toddlers a hoot? At one or two they're just getting their legs, and then they can *run!* *(Openly eat your candy bar. Don't share. Pretend like this is normal. Make sure the rest of the candy is well hidden.)*

Toddlers have no fear. They will try anything and think nothing bad will ever happen. My friend's toddler is named Matthew. She used to take him to a Christian school where she taught journalism. He livened that class up! Well, one day he soaked his entire outfit with spilled apple juice. By the end of class, she'd had to strip him down to his diaper and sneakers! He had the cutest pot belly and was just happy to run around like that.

Well, that day, Mom and Matthew headed to the car. Suddenly, Matthew snatched a candy bar from one of the students and took off. Everybody laughed as the naked baby ran off holding his new candy bar high. Mom was in hot pursuit—but a toddler with a candy bar can move!

He wanted to *keep* that candy bar! *(Shake your half-eaten candy bar at them.)*

Well, everybody laughed. Baby runs. Mom chases. Kids laugh some more. Round and round the cars they went. Matthew loved it! The kids loved it!

But Mom did not love it. For she saw something her baby—and the other kids—did not see.

A truck. *(Pause. Look around. Your audience should be properly horrified. Mine actually gasped.)*

I know! But still that baby ran. All he could see was the melting candy in his fist. The kids saw only fun.

Luckily, at the last minute, the driver saw Baby Matthew. The truck stopped in time. And sweating mightily, Mom scooped up her baby and muttered a big thank you to God.

None of us likes to admit it—not even us big kids!—but parents often know when trouble is coming. Parents have seen trouble. They know trucks often zoom into empty parking lots. They've seen some horrible, sad things. And they don't want to see them again. They want their sons and daughters safe because they love them very, very much.

God gave each of us parents to care for us. And God himself is our Father too. We need to stop and hear what our parents have to say. We need to honor them by listening.

We all like to be heard. And just like our Father in heaven, our parents truly care for us. They don't just make crazy rules to spoil our fun—to keep us from chocolate and wild chases. They want to keep us safe.

Let's pray. *(Ask a child to pray or use the following.)* Father, I don't always understand rules. I don't always like them. But help me to hear, Lord. Open my ears to those who love me, especially those who take care of me. Their words have more value than a quick trip or treat. I know that parents—and you, loving Father—always want the best for me. Even if I can't see it coming. Amen. *(Hand out candy bars.)*

Grumpy and Sleepy

The Point of It All

We all have moods. How can you accept yours and use them? Can you commit never to let the sun set on your anger?

Objects

A favorite book—*Snow White and the Seven Dwarfs* if you have it

Pair of sneakers, jump rope, pine cone—whatever represents activities in which you are interested

Bible with tea bag or packet of hot chocolate tucked near your favorite verse

Unpopped bag of popcorn or similar soothing treat

Small pillow

If you're up to it, wear a cap (like the seven dwarfs) or scrunch and mash your hair to make it look like you have "bedhead." You could even wear some dowdy pajamas.

To Dos

Pray and journal about what comforts you.

Think about the last time you blew up when grumpy or tired. How did you make amends? How did you resolve to do better next time? What tools did you discover? Think about the last time you were grumpy or tired and handled it better. What did you do? Lie down? Take a nap? Take a walk? Read your Bible? Say the Lord's Prayer or count to ten? We all have God-given emotions—especially the "creative" among us. How do you handle yours? You might find something original to share that will help the many exhausted servants in your church.

Select a few accomplices in the audience. Ask them to push their purse or bag out into the aisle, get in your way, talk, etc.—anything you can "grump" about.

Verses to Pray On

Psalm 4:4–5

Be angry, and do not sin. Meditate within your heart on your bed, and be still. Offer the sacrifices of righteousness, and put your trust in the LORD.

Proverbs 15:1

A soft answer turns away wrath, but a harsh word stirs up anger.

Ephesians 4:26–27

Be angry, and do not sin: do not let the sun go down on your wrath, nor give place to the devil.

Ready, Set, Go!

(Amble down the aisle as if half asleep. Scratch your head. Mumble. If a child looks frightened, wink at him or her as if you share a secret. As you pass your accomplices, stumble over their purse or bump into them. Mutter at them, maybe even give them a gentle push. Grump a little at a few kids in your audience.) Good morning! Ha! Who thought that up? I am so tired. Hey! Stop talking! What was I saying? Oh dear, I'm sooo tired. I don't know why I have to be here today! Hey, be quiet—I have a headache! I shouldn't have even come today! *(When finished complaining, smile—big! Make sure your accomplices smile big too. Exchange glances, smiles, or winks to assure the kids. Some children—and adults—are truly frightened by anger of any kind.)*

How would you feel if I didn't show up or if I grumped at you like it was your fault I was having a bad day? It would feel awful, wouldn't it? My friends volunteered to "take" my grumpiness without shoving back, but it's not something they need or deserve, is it? *(Pause.)*

And yet we all get grumpy. Angry. Moody. It's part of how God made us. Even Christ got angry—like when he cleared the moneychangers out of the temple. Remember? Jesus chased them out of his "church" and tossed their tables and chairs upside down! Remember what he did next? He invited the blind and the lame in to heal them. His anger was important there.

Christ understands that we get angry. And God gave us feelings to protect us from danger and to cry off sadness. So what do we do with feelings when they might hurt others?

(Hold up each object as you talk about it—sneakers for walks, pillow for naps, a pine cone for nature.) I take walks. I warn my family that I'm feeling grumpy and tired. I'm still responsible for how I act, but that helps them be a little kinder to me, because that's what I need. Sometimes I take naps or eat a snack. I go outside and look at nature. I read a good book or my favorite Bible verse with a cup of tea.

I would never do what I did today—especially in church. *(Wink and giggle.)* No one would. But behind closed doors can be very different. In fact, if I walked in here in the middle of a huff, I'd quickly fix it! So that tells me I can control it. I just need to love God and my family enough to control it at home too. I need to find places to express my feelings safely, because just a few angry words or pushes can start a great big argument, can't they? But the Bible says in several places, "Be angry, and do not sin." *Be* angry. *And* do not sin. Both. Why? Because God gave us anger. He knows we need it sometimes. And he knows sometimes we goof up or yell at people.

And nobody deserves that! I don't. And neither do you. Let's treat others with love and work on coaxing the Sleepy and Grumpy out of us before we do something else.

Let's pray. *(Ask a child to pray or use the following.)* Father, I know you understand my moods. Teach me how to use them. Help me use the strength of anger to sweep the porch or take out the trash. Remind me to use the exhaustion of sadness for a good nap and to use the depth of sorrow to write or to call someone. Remind me that perfection is not even possible. If it was, we wouldn't need you, Jesus. Now that would be sad! Amen.

Knock, Knock! Who's There?

The Point of It All

Knock and God will answer.

Objects

Bible

Note card, with basic outline of sermon and sequence
of jokes, hidden in your Bible

Bob the Puppet

To Dos

Practice until you see Bob as a "real boy."

Practice mumbling through your favorite prayer at
record speed.

Verses to Pray On

Luke 11:1–13, especially verse 9:

*So I say to you, ask, and it will be given to you; seek, and
you will find; knock, and it will be opened to you.*

Ready, Set, Go!

Hi, guys! Having a great day? *(Pause.)* I want to introduce
you to a friend of mine. He has wanted to come and join us
here for some time now, but he has a little self-control problem. He isn't grown up like you guys, and he interrupts *all*

the time. And he has a *horrible* habit—he talks in knock-knock jokes!

You: Well, are you ready, Bob? Do you think you can do it?

Bob: *(Nods vigorously.)* Ready, yup, yup, ready! *(Ad lib a weird noise or occasionally hit a squeaker. Our puppet growls and purrs like Yoda from* Star Wars.*)*

You: All right. Don't get too excited now. Today, Bob, we're going to talk about prayer. You know, Bob, there was a time in my life when I would speed through my prayers, bowing only on one knee—it was a launch pad! I was in such a hurry to stand up and get going. Let me give you an example. *(Say a bedtime prayer or the Lord's Prayer at record speed.)* What do you think God thought of that? *(Pause.)* I just didn't have any time to talk to God back then. I was so busy doing . . . doing—well, I was doing something!

Bob: *(Interrupting)* Knock, knock!

You: Now, Bob, I thought you weren't going to interrupt today. Well, OK. Who's there?

Bob: Foyer! Foyer! Foyer's there! Foyer!

You: Foyer who?

Bob: Foyer information, I pray every day—without ceasing! Yuk, yuk, yuk! *(Bob throws his head back and laughs loudly and obnoxiously, shaking with wide-open mouth.)*

You: Good, Bob, good. OK now, shhh. Remember what we talked about. So *(turn back to kids)*, when we pray, we want to pray as Jesus taught us and take our time. *Talk* to God. Jesus said if we just ask, we'll receive. If we just seek, we'll find. Just like the game only better. God doesn't hide when we seek. He's right there! Jesus also said, "To him who knocks it will be opened."

Bob: *(Interrupting)* Knock, knock!

You: *(Look at kids and roll your eyes.)* Not that kind of knocking, Bob! OK, OK. Who's there?

Bob: Karen! Karen! Karen's there! Karen!

You: *(Sigh deeply.)* Karen who?

Bob: Karen and sharin' are great ways to show God's love! Yuk, yuk, yuk! *(Loud, bobbing back and forth.)* Knock, knock!

You: Bob, this is the last one now. Who's there?

Bob: Wooden shoe. *(Looks at kids and then at pastor. Quick, sharp head movement.)*

You: Wooden shoe who?

Bob: Wooden shoe love it if I stopped interrupting? Ahh, yuk, yuk, yuk!

You: *(Laugh.)* Why yes, Bob, that would be wonderful! Oh my! *(Turn to kids.)* So what happens when we knock on God's door in prayer? *(Pause.)* That's right—he answers. He always answers. He has promised it, and he always keeps his word!

Bob: *(Interrupting)* Knock, knock!

You: *(Shake head and smile at kids.)* Bob! Oh, I give up! Who's there?

Bob: Freddie! Freddie! Freddie! *(You start to speak. Bob cuts you off with a sharp snap of his head in your direction. Sigh heavily.)* Freddie!

You: Freddie? Now, Bob . . . OK. Freddie who?

Bob: Freddie or not, it's time to go! Yuk, yuk, yuk!

You: *(Laugh, turn to kids.)* Well, this time he's right. Thank you for being so good, guys. Bob, we're going to have to work together on some things, OK?

Let's pray. *(Ask a child to pray or use the following.)* Father, you never play games. When we seek, you never hide. When we knock, you always answer. I'm glad you're there for us! Amen.

Note: Puppets may seem a bit intimidating, but this routine was the first one to really work for me. It allowed me to focus mostly on the children. It also gave them a chance to be "more mature" than the interrupting puppet. Adults and kids loved it.

Don't worry about whether your lips move; it doesn't matter, because the audience will be completely focused on the puppet. Just make sure Bob is prepared when you approach the children. He must be "alive" every moment they see him.

Man on the Moon

The Point of It All

Jesus said we should be a light. But some people can only see darkness in the world. Only God can reach them.

Objects

Toy rocket
Small American flag on a stick
Bible

To Dos

Reflect on the stories or your own memories of man landing on the moon. Have you ever met anyone who doubted it? Can you and I prove it? It takes faith in science, NASA, and media reports. It all *could* have been a hoax. We just agree that the science and the agencies involved are valid, but we *personally* can't prove man's trip to the moon to a true doubter. Nor can we prove the existence of God. But we don't doubt him either!

Verses to Pray On

Matthew 5:14–16

You are the light of the world. A city that is set on a hill cannot be hidden. . . . Let your light so shine before men, that they may see your good works and glorify your Father in heaven.

Matthew 7:8–9

Everyone who asks receives, and he who seeks finds, and to him who knocks it will be opened. Or what man is there among you who, if his son asks for bread, will give him a stone?

Ready, Set, Go!

(Sit down—or run around—and play "Zoom! Zoom!" with the rocket. Pretend it flies and shout, "Zoom! Zoom!")
   Oh *(suddenly notice the kids with a smile)*, isn't this great? I love rockets and astronauts and watching God's great big universe twinkle over my house every night. It's a miracle, isn't it? Truly God's work!
   When I was five years old *(personalize this)* man walked on the moon. *The moon!* They even left an American flag there, because America was the first to make it. *(Wave flag.)*
   It was a very big deal. Do you believe it really happened? *(Pause.)* You know what? Some people don't believe it. They think it was just a silly trick made up like an old Hollywood movie. But most people *do* believe it happened. I

108

saw the moon launch on TV, and I've visited the exhibits in museums and looked at bits and pieces of moon rocks those astronauts picked up and brought back. What a souvenir, huh? To me, this is enough proof. I believe it. But every once in a while I'll meet somebody who says, *"Prove man walked on the moon!"*

The fact is, I can't prove it. I can give them books to read, tell them what I saw on TV, take them to a museum, even rent a movie for them. But I can't really prove it.

If they don't believe in the proof—I can't change that for them.

In a way, our belief in God is like that. All religions agree that Christ walked the earth and that he was a good man and a teacher. History proves it. But many say he was just "a really nice guy." Some people don't believe that Jesus is the Son of God, that he rose and walked the earth for *forty days* after his death, and that he ascended into heaven to prepare a home for us.

I can give them books to read *(hold up Bible)*, tell them what I've seen, take them to church, even rent videos for them. I can even share miracles I have seen—miracles in my family and friends. Miracles in my own life! But really, if these nonbelievers don't believe, I can't make them. That's sad, isn't it? *(Pause.)*

You know what, though? We can pray for them. We can ask God to do what we can't—and he can! Dare doubters to do the same. Dare them to ask God to show up and prove himself. He can, and he will—maybe through their friends, a loved one, or even their own miracle. If they knock, God will answer. And he'll be creative about it too!

Let's pray. *(Ask a child to pray or use the following.)* Father, help us be a light to the world. But with those doubters who refuse to believe, please take over for us. Please hold them and love them, and give them what they need, so that they may feel your love. Amen.

An "I" Infection

The Point of It All

We all need to be on time with God's work. If we jump ahead or put off doing God's plans, we may miss our chance.

Objects

Eye patch—could be an adhesive bandage or cotton with tape

Watch or clock

Hot dog—or something that has to do with what you do right after church

To Dos

Get eye patch ready to put on at appropriate time.

Rest and pray on God's meaning of this message for you. Are you right on time with God's will? Rushing? Doing his work for him? Procrastinating out of fear or busyness?

Review anything stagnating or bothering you right now. You may find an answer for *you!* Of course, you may be right on time. I'm usually patient with one project but need a "Whoa, Nelly!" or a "Giddy Up" on another—all in the same day!

Verses to Pray On

Ecclesiastes 3, especially verse 1:

To everything there is a season, a time for every purpose under heaven.

Ready, Set, Go!

(Put eye patch on out of sight of children.) Hi, guys! It's good to see you! You know, this morning I had an I-I-I infection. I needed your help so badly. And, you see, I wanted to see you, so I came right to church. That's right! Got dressed, ate breakfast, read my Bible, and drove right over. The sun wasn't up, but I was here. I was so excited! *(Dangle the clock or watch.)*

You're not going to believe this, but you weren't here! *(Pause and look surprised.)* The lights were off, and it was chilly in here. And dark. I was alone, but I did my little sermon anyway. After all, I was so excited!

And I have to tell you, I was mighty disappointed in all of you. *(Grin to the wee ones so they know you're kidding.)* Here I was, ready to go, all my stuff ready, and you didn't show up. *(Pause.)* Well, yes, that was five hours ago. You were just getting up! You couldn't even hear all the great stuff I talked about, could you?

I'm teasing, of course. I wasn't here. But what if I'd rushed over and done it my way? After church I usually go home and fix hot dogs for our family. *(Hold up hot dog or whatever you brought.)* I would already be taking my Sunday afternoon nap by now! *(Snore loudly.)* And you'd be here. Alone!

That would be very sad, wouldn't it? I did have an I-I-I infection. *I* wanted to get started. *I* was excited. *I* went ahead. *I* did what *I* wanted! And I forgot about you. I forgot about God's plans for all of us! That *is* an "I" infection,

111

isn't it? I-I-I—that's all I *(emphasize and point to self)* could think about. Some people call it a Me-Me morning. *(Sing like tuning your voice, "Me, me, me, me, me!")* I just keep singing on about me, me, me, and what I want.

God's timing is important. He sets things up for a reason. Sometimes I have to wait for something special—like Christmas. Or I have to wait for something I want—even to come to church and be with you. But when it finally comes—on God's time, not mine—it's a wonderful time!

Let's pray. *(Ask a child to pray or use the following.)* Father, help us pray for your perfect timing. Help us to be on time for *you*. Amen.

Mind Your own Business!

The Point of It All

If we could mind our own business, we would have a lot more time to do God's work. And our own!

Objects

Bob the Puppet (see introduction)

To Dos

Practice with Bob.

Verses to Pray On

Matthew 12:37

> *For by your words you will be justified,*
> *and by your words you will be condemned.*

112

1 Timothy 5:13

They learn to be idle, wandering about from house to house, and not only idle but also gossips and busybodies, saying things which they ought not.

Ready, Set, Go!

Look who I brought! Bob "Who's There?" the Puppet. Glad you could visit, Bob! Say hello to the kids, Bob.

Bob: Hellooo to the kids, Bob. Yuk, yuk, yuk!

You: Bob, you're so silly! Just say hello! You're acting like a dummy!

Bob: Dummy! Look who's calling whom a dummy!

You: Bob! You are not showing the proper respect. You're so rude! You must be exhausted! That's no excuse, but I know you've been awfully busy lately.

Bob: Yes, I am exhausted. Just like my bike.

You: Your bike? *(Look confused. Look at kids and back at Bob.)*

Bob: Yeah. It's two tired. Get it—two tired? Yuk, yuk, yuk, yuk!

You: *(Shake your head at the kids and smirk.)*

Bob: Yeah, yeah. And I'm seeing spots. I'm so *tired* I'm seeing spots!

You: Spots! Bob, have you seen a doctor?

Bob: No, just spots. Yuk, yuk, yuk, yuk!

You: All right, seriously now, why are you so tired? And no bicycle jokes, please. *(Roll your eyes at the kids as if Bob's jokes are awful. This will build a distance between you and Bob, making him more alive. And it will bring kinship between you and the kids, and allow all to laugh at the silliness.)*

Bob: Well, lately I've been in the mining business.

You: Gold? You're mining gold? Now that's just silly, Bob!

Bob: No, the mining business. I'm mining the business of everybody in town. Yuk, yuk, yuk!

You: Well, that can be exhausting!

Bob: Yeah, well everybody needs my help. When my friends have troubles, I gotta tell them what to do. Settle their arguments. Help them. And when they get it wrong—all the time!—I need to help them again. And I gotta call my other friends all the time to let them know what's going on so they can help too. And they give me more problems to solve. And by the time we're done gossiping, I mean *(cough, cough—roll your eyes at the kids)*, praying about it all, I'm completely exhausted. We say great prayers: "Lord, help Patty not be so mean. Lord, help Danny not to be such a lazy loser. Father, change my mom so she lets me have two desserts—as any good mom would!" It's all so much work, I don't even have time for my new sales job.

You: Hmm. A new sales job—now that sounds positive.

Bob: Yeah, it would be. But so far I'm too busy to do much work. And I only got two orders all week.

You: Two isn't bad. What were they?

Bob: Yeah. "Get out!" and "Stay out!" Yuk, yuk, yuk!

You: You're a mess, Bob. You might get better "orders" if you began to mind your own business. Why don't you try praying about that? And how about if you just encouraged your friends instead of sharing their business and telling them what to do? Would that make your life any easier?

Bob: What? Well, who are *you* to tell *me* what to do? I've even had to pray for *you*, you know. You are such a busybody! And you know the Bible is against that. You know, _____ *(your name)*, you should really put more effort into your Christian walk, 'cause your talk is just a mess. Like I was telling Suzanna Smith the other day, "If _____ *(your name)* would just mind her own business, she sure would have time to do her job. I was saying—" *(At this point, stuff Bob under your arm.)*

You: Good-bye, Bob! *(Roll your eyes at the kids again.)* Sometimes the only way to stop bad talk is to stop listening to it. Let's pray and go, boys and girls. I think Bob needs to go home and think about it all. He's a talker but not such a good listener, huh? Two ears and one mouth—I wonder what God meant by making us like that? What do you think? *(Pause.)*

Let's pray. *(Ask a child to pray or use the following.)* Father, help us to hear others. Help us to mind our own business. Help us to live lives you are proud of. And when we're tempted to gossip, please close our mouths and remind us to open our ears. Amen.

open Your Gifts

The Point of It All

We all have gifts we have buried or ignored. Why?

Objects

Huge gift bag or box. Make it as pretty as possible—as if a costly gift is inside. Then beat it around a bit. Rip it. Drag it in the dirt. Put baby powder or dust on it. Do whatever it takes to make it look old and neglected.

Fill the bag or box with things you can pass out—pencils, gum, candy, or trinkets from fast-food kids' meals. If you do this near a holiday, you may want to have fun going "bigger." The better the gifts, the better the effect!

I actually brought my guitar (see below), made it dusty, and stretched a fake spider web across the top. I bought the spider web at a dollar store after Halloween.

To Dos

Pray and journal. What unfulfilled dreams do you have? I once wanted to run a "Good News" newspaper. At the time, I was a stay-at-home mom writing for a local newspaper. I had no experience in managing a newspaper. Since then I've been blessed to work in a large newsroom, start a school newspaper, and now run a teen magazine (www.teenlight.org). I didn't realize the connection until this year! I still want to learn to play the guitar. Yet I only pick up my beautiful guitar to dust it. (Not often—ha!) It's an unopened gift for me that would add to my life and ministry. I can't tell you what's holding me back! I'm busy, but I still find time for other things. How about you? We must honor God with our mind—continue to grow—if we are to be happy and fulfilled.

Verses to Pray On

1 Timothy 4:14–15

Do not neglect the gift that is in you, which was given to you by prophecy with the laying on of the hands of the eldership. Meditate on these things; give yourself entirely to them, that your progress may be evident to all.

2 Timothy 1:6–9

Therefore I remind you to stir up the gift of God which is in you through the laying on of my hands. For God has not given us a sprit of fear, but of power and of love and of a sound mind. Therefore do not be ashamed of the testimony of our Lord, nor of me His prisoner, but share with me in the sufferings for the gospel according to the power of God, who has saved us and called us with a holy calling, not according to our works, but according to His own purpose and grace which was given to us in Christ Jesus before time began.

Ready, Set, Go!

How are you doing? What a special day this is! *(Place the enormous gift between you and the children.)* What do you think of this beautiful gift? It's lovely, isn't it? *(Pause.)*

Well, it *was* lovely. I'm sure it's still nice inside. I guess. I've never looked inside. Hey, I've never looked inside! *(Pause and look at them. Hopefully they'll urge you on.)* Should I look? Would you look? It's a gift from my father. He often asks me how I like his gifts, how I'm enjoying them. I usually just talk about something else. I don't want to admit that my gift is still sitting in my closet.

(Get excited again.) But it's such a beautiful gift—I just had to show it to you! What do you say? Want to help me open it? I know my father meant me to—OK! Help me!

(Open the bag or box and pass out the trinkets.) Oh, let's share it all! Here, I think it was really meant for *all* of us. I have such a great father, don't I? He really loves me. He wants us all to be happy!

What was I afraid of? *(Pause.)* You know, sometimes I treat God's gifts this way. God will give me a gift *(describe yours—giving, singing, preaching, teaching, baking, etc.)* and I hesitate to use it—to open and share my gift. I even felt nervous when I was asked to do the teaching here at church. What is *that* about?

I guess it's just normal to be afraid sometimes, especially of something new. But the apostle Paul said this: "Do not neglect the gift that is in you." He said to think about that gift, pray about it, and *give yourself to the gift.* Then everybody will see it in you. For example, if you're a singer, open your mouth and sing. If you want to write, pick up a pencil. Bake an elderly person some cookies. Get going! It feels great—because God built you *for* those gifts. And everybody will see your gift and know that it's from God. Neat, huh?

Let's pray. *(Ask a child to pray or use the following.)* Father, your gifts are tremendous. Beautiful. I don't want to let them go to waste, to turn to dust. Help me to kick out the fear and bring on the gift! Amen.

Role Call

The Point of It All

Do you have any idea what the life of your pastor is like? How can you appreciate your pastor fully if you don't understand all that your pastor does? Do this sermon as a surprise—just as most of his midnight distress calls are a surprise.

Objects

Gifts for your pastor that represent his or her many roles. (See ideas in lesson.) Make it personal. If your pastor is active in the music program, a CD is a good idea. All pastors are teachers, so an apple is great! Maybe you will want to give bandages to represent healing the sick or a rubber band for being pulled in many directions and never breaking.

Basket to hold the gifts—either to present to the pastor or to be returned to you for another day.

To Dos

Choose a dependable, reserved (calm) child to present the pastor's gifts as you speak. If you don't have one old enough, choose a friend to help. Make sure the gifts are labeled and the volunteer knows when to present them.

Pray about, or discuss with a close friend, whether there are others you should honor along with your pastor.

Prepare the gifts. Try to work with the Sunday school teachers. Ask them to prepare cards or gifts for the pastor. Start the week before so they have time to prepare.

Verses to Pray On

Proverbs 26:2

Like a flitting sparrow, like a flying swallow,
So a curse without cause shall not alight.

Matthew 10:40–41

He who receives you receives Me, and he who receives Me
receives Him who sent Me. He who receives a prophet in
the name of a prophet shall receive a prophet's reward.
And he who receives a righteous man in the name of a
righteous man shall receive a righteous man's reward.

Ready, Set, Go!

It's good to see you! It's good to see our pastor too, isn't it? Let's all say "Hi!" Ready? Say it with me. One, two, three: Hi, Pastor _____! He's (She's) the best, isn't he (she)?

Well, today is not Pastor Appreciation Day, but we want to thank our pastor every day, don't we? So why not today? Let's thank our pastor for all he (she) is! *(Again, you'll have to personalize this.)* Ours is a pastor, a husband, a father, a grandfather. *(Pause between each role as your volunteer presents the corresponding gift. Gifts may include a book, a gift certificate to a nice restaurant, a framed photo, a disposable camera, etc.)* When we look at all our pastor's jobs in one place, we realize that he's (she's) a busy person! Yet it never shows. Pastor _____ just gladly goes around tending to the sick, helping the poor, hugging the sad. We only get a peek at what he (she) does. I'm sure we'll never know even the half of it.

And Pastor _____ never complains—even if we do. *(If you're brave, make a guilty face. People do judge pastors and their families harshly.)*

120

We have a lot to be grateful for, don't we? *(Pause. Make sure the children have presented their gifts.)* Let's have a round of applause for our pastor and his (her) family! We are truly blessed. It's easy to forget that—especially when people are so good at what they do that you barely notice. After all, if your mom always does the laundry or your sister always does the dishes, who notices? It's only when there are dirty socks and gloppy dishes of old mashed potatoes all around that anybody thinks about them.

Let's notice. Let's all say, "Thank you for all you do!" Ready? *(Motion to those in the pews too!)* One, two, three: "Thank you for all you do!" *(If not very loud or impressive, cue them again with a smile.)*

Let's pray. *(Ask a child to pray or use the following.)* Father, you have blessed us with a wonderful leader, teacher, pastor, and friend in Pastor _____. Thank you, Father. Please bless Pastor _____, and remind us to show our appreciation every day. Amen.

BBQ Your Enemies

The Point of It All

We all have enemies. What can we pray to protect us from consuming resentment? The "enemy" sleeps soundly while our minds race. So whom are we destroying?

Objects

Bag of charcoal
Plate covered in foil
Candy or cake that can be broken in half

To Dos

Get an accomplice to gossip and complain about your enemy (see lesson).

Think of three things you'd like to have. Then think of someone who has been just horrible to you, someone who has truly betrayed you. Now pray that God will give the three things you desire to them.

Journal about what hate and resentment do to your day. Yesterday resentment made me late two times. I got lost reliving an insulting event that wasn't worth my time when it happened. Yet I went there again and again.

When I do get lost in resentment (God must expect it or he wouldn't provide a map to show us the way out!), I try to remember to pray for my enemies, because God has promised that my kindness will "heap coals of fire" on their heads.

Verses to Pray On

Proverbs 25:21–22

If your enemy is hungry, give him bread to eat;
And if he is thirsty, give him water to drink;
For so you will heap coals of fire on his head,
And the LORD will reward you.

Matthew 5:44–46

But I say to you, love your enemies, bless those who curse you, do good to those who hate you, and pray for those who spitefully use you and persecute you, that you may be sons of your Father in heaven; for He makes His sun rise on the evil and on the good, and sends rain on the just and on the unjust. For if you love those who love you, what reward have you? Do not even the tax collectors do the same?

Ready, Set, Go!

(Act preoccupied. Halfway down the aisle, stop and whisper to a friend. Shake your head in disgust. Loudly say, "Can you believe she did that?") Hi. I'm not even sure I can do this today. I am *so* angry. You wouldn't believe what happened to me last night! I haven't slept all night! I am just too upset, too tired, and too angry to even do this today. I'm sorry, but I'm sure you understand.

(Get up and leave the stage in a storm. Just before exiting, turn and smile.) Just kidding. But I hate to admit it, I've had days like that. Really, people can be so mean. They say cruel things and hurt you on purpose. It's hard to get over that. It can ruin your whole day, even your whole week. Some poor souls allow it to ruin a lifetime!

But let's pretend that a neighbor came over to my house last night and really insulted me. Called me crazy. Called me stupid. *(Pause with eyes wide.)* Said the dinner I fixed was stinky. Made fun of my hair. Even said my dog was *ugly* and had fleas. Well, I tell you, I just could not believe it! I had to call my best friend and tell her all about it. Oh, wait, that's right—we're making this up! *(Widen eyes, grin, and giggle. Pretend you were caught up in the anger again.)*

Now, people do bad things sometimes. Those things are wrong. *(Pause.)* And sometimes we do have actual enemies, don't we, or God wouldn't talk about how to treat them, right? *(Pause.)* But God doesn't want us to be filled with hate or resentment toward them. He wants us to have peace.

So guess what God says to do to your enemy? You get to "heap coals of fire on his head, and the LORD will reward you." Ha! No kidding. That's Proverbs 25:22. Do you know how? No, don't empty out your barbecue grill on their head, silly! *(Hold up charcoals. Drop them as if hot.)*

It's much smarter than that. Here's how. Ready? Listening? *(Tug on your ear. Wait for full attention.)* "If your enemy is hungry, give him bread to eat; and if he is thirsty, give him water to drink." *(As you talk, hold up what you brought to share.)*

If your neighbor seems crabby or complains over nothing, bring him an extra plate from a church supper. Just drop it off and say, "Thought you might enjoy this." Simple. Smile and leave. Bring her an extra flower from a beautiful bush in your yard. Wave hi when you really want to *yell* something else.

How about that kid at the lunch table who drives you crazy? Talk over a plan with your parents. Maybe bring an extra treat for lunch and toss it over to him. *(Hold up the prop you brought.)* Just smile and pray silently for him. Pray that God would bless him.

The point? Jesus wants *you* to have peace. He wants *you* to be safe. And if we continually go over the bad things in life, we feel bad. Our enemies are at the movies or playing with friends while our minds spin with hate and payback plans.

We're God's kids. He wants much, much more than hate and trouble for us. He wants us to experience freedom and joy. Pray for *that* for your enemies. You'll find it for yourself.

After all, God is an excellent Father. He *never* breaks his promises.

Let's pray. *(Ask a child to pray or use the following.)* Father, please take care of our enemies. Bring them peace, joy, and happiness. Remind me that I may easily have the same. And when I forget, or when they attack again—which they may—remind me to pray. I'm worth that. Far more than that. Thanks for knowing me so well, Father. Amen.

Remember to Forget

The Point of It All

We often remember a slight or an insult over all else.

Objects

Calendar or daily planner
Post-It notes with "reminders" written on them
Pen
Bright ribbon or string tied on finger
Something written on the back of your hand
Large mirror

To Dos

Prepare the above.
Pray about the message. Do you remember to forget?

Verse to Pray On

Colossians 3:13

Even as Christ forgave you, so you also must do.

Ready, Set, Go!

I am so forgetful. I write everything I have to do on this calendar: when it's my son's turn to bring snacks to school, when I have an appointment at the doctor's office, even when I promise to call someone to see how they're doing. Birthdays, holidays—it all goes in here. I don't even know what day Easter is this year, do you? *(Personalize this.)*

And if I'm not near the calendar and something important pops up, I write it on my hand. See? And I stick these things *(hold up a messy pile of Post-Its)* all over my computer to remember things. It looks like a big puzzle. Ha! Sometimes it is!

What types of things do you forget? *(Pause.)* Me too! I forget to take out the trash. I used to stay up late and do all my homework and then leave it on the counter at home. Big zero! Ouch!

How about when you're angry with someone—do you forget that? You know, like a friend takes a special toy, or won't share, or says something mean, mean, *mean* and later apologizes. Do you forget about it?

I have to admit, I don't know how to forget those things. I'm working on it though. Even when I've decided that I forgive them, even when I promise them and God that I forgive them, sometimes I really don't. Oh, I'm OK for a while. Kind. Sweet. We're friends. But then something else happens and I pull my resentment back out and hold it against them, kind of like this mirror. *(Hold mirror up to them, but make sure the reflection faces you.)*

Only the mirror doesn't really reflect them; they've already done all they can to change the past. And the truth is, nobody can really change the past. Nobody.

Do you know who the mirror really reflects? *(Pause.)* That's right! It only shows me. Just like my resentment. It only shows me—that I never really forgave them. That I'm saving that stuff up for the next time I need it. You know, to throw back at them later. Does it keep me safe, make me better, or save me next time I do something stinky or mean? Something inside of me thinks it will help me, but God knows better. He wants more for me.

I want to learn to forget. Really forget. And the next time I try to hold one little event against a person, I want to remember something good she did instead.

Hey, maybe I need a Post-It note for that!

OK, let's pray. *(Ask a child to pray or use the following.)* Father, help me to remember to forget the bad. And could you help me to remember my homework and to take out the trash too? Amen.

A Round of Prayer

The Point of It All

Committing to prayer really can change the world. Just praying for seconds at a stoplight can make a difference, and it's a great way to spend the time too!

Objects

Copies of the following song to pass out to the kids (or use an overhead transparency); sing to the tune of "Row, Row, Row Your Boat"
>   Pray, pray, pray, my dear
>   For friends and fam-i-ly,
>   Pray and pray and pray some more,
>   How happy we will be!

To Dos

Practice the song above.

It's best if the kids can practice the song in Sunday school. At least ask three older children to practice and act as leaders of the rounds.

127

Pray about whether you keep commitments to pray for others. When you say, "I'll pray for you," do you? What does "Pray without ceasing" mean to you? Is it possible? Desirable? Is this exhortation aimed only at a few?

Verse to Pray On

1 Thessalonians 5:17

Pray without ceasing.

Ready, Set, Go!

I've waited all week to see you! In fact, I feel so good I need to sing! *(Try to sing the word* sing.*)* In fact, I knew I'd feel this good, so I have a song for all of us to sing! *(Have one of the older kids pass out the song or project it on a screen.)*

This song is about prayer. Praying, praying, praying— for friends and family. Do you know that the apostle Paul said we should pray *all* the time? Without stopping! Do you think he meant for me to drive here with my eyes closed and my hands folded on top of the steering wheel? *(Pause for answers.)*

I think you're right. So what *did* he mean? *(Pause.)* That's right! I bet you whisper prayers all day. "Thanks, God, for my brother." *(Laugh and wink.)* "Please help me with this test." Then there are the really good prayers: "Dear God, please help Grandma get better." "Help my dog come home." "Take care of Aunt Mary as she flies home." "Help my friend to feel better."

Talking to God is simple. You know the best prayer? "Help." That's it: "Help!" After all, God knows how to take care of *everything!*

Well, what if the skies were filled with the sounds of children and adults praying—whispered love notes to God, prayers for good things, prayers of thanksgiving? I think it would sound like choruses of angels singing, which got me to thinking—we need a song!

Let's sing it. (*Sing.*)

That was beautiful. Was it perfect? (*Pause.*) You're right. Was it still beautiful? Yes, it was! Thank you for that glorious blessing. I feel even better! Wow!

Let's pray. (*Ask a child to pray or use the following.*) Father, teach me to pray throughout the day. Whispered bits of thanks and prayers for help will improve my day and make me more aware of your love and care. Thanks! Amen.

Squeaky Clean Mud Puddles

The Point of It All

We all sin every day. How can we blend gratitude, love, self-esteem, and righteousness into a healthy walk with our Father?

Objects

Soap
Washcloth

To Dos

Pray and journal about the balance between guilt and the freedom of forgiveness. We all tend to lean one way or the other. How can we teach the children (and the parents) a healthy balance? How can we teach them to avoid sin yet have healthy self-esteem? How can we reassure them that they are loved and valued by our Maker and Father—no matter what?

Verses to Pray On

Hebrews 9:14

How much more shall the blood of Christ, who through the eternal Spirit offered Himself without spot to God, cleanse your conscience from dead works to serve the living God?

Hebrews 10:10, 14

By that will we have been sanctified through the offering of the body of Jesus Christ once for all. . . . For by one offering He has perfected forever those who are being sanctified.

Ready, Set, Go!

Do you take baths? *(Pause.)* Showers? *(Pause.)* When you do a good job—behind the ears and everything *(mimic motions with washcloth; you might want to squeak as you wash your ears)*—you're squeaky clean, right?

But as the day goes on, you might splash in the mud or trip and fall in the dirt. You might get jelly on your shirt or bright red marker on your fingers.

You were really, really careful all day. But by dinner time—maybe by lunch!—you have dirty smudges on your clothes or skin just from living life. Hardly any of them were on purpose. You didn't mean to get them. Well, maybe the mud puddle was on purpose! *(Grin.)*

Did you know that sin is the same way? *(Pause.)* Try to go just one day without sin. Just one day. Try it! I have. I always end up judging someone or having pride—pride that I didn't sin that day! Ha!

God knows his children. He knows we'll jump in the mud once in a while or forget to use a napkin. He loves us, so he wipes us clean. He gives us a bath, makes us clean, showers us in blessings of forgiveness. And all we need to do is pray and ask God for forgiveness. We need to try hard to avoid the puddles, of course, but God will take care of each and every smudge. We just need to ask.

Let's pray. *(Ask a child to pray or use the following.)* Father, I do sin. I don't want to, I try hard not to, but I do. Please help me to share your boundless love and forgiveness with others. Help me to concentrate on how much love you must have to take away every spot. Amen.

The Bea-u-ti-ful, Bounti-ful Be-atti-tudes

The Point of It All

Do we really understand some of the "fancy" words in the Bible? What do the Beatitudes mean to you?

Objects

Dictionary
Bible

To Dos

Practice pronouncing *Be-attitudes* (Beatitudes) so it will stick with the kids.

Read the Beatitudes and the dictionary definition of the word. Journal or pray about what they mean to you. If you find something good, share it in your sermon.

Verses to Pray On

Luke 6:20–38

The Beatitudes

Ready, Set, Go!

Oh! It is so bea-u-ti-ful to see you this bea-u-ti-ful day! Speaking of bea-u-ti-ful, have you ever heard of the Be-attitudes? You know, the Beatitudes in the New Testament? *(Pause.)* That's right, that *is* a great big bea-u-ti-ful word, isn't it? It sounds like "Be attitude," doesn't it?

The Beatitudes were part of a talk Jesus had with his disciples after he had healed a lot of people one day. He talked about the blessings that the poor, the hungry, the sad, and the hated would be given through God. Jesus begins, "Blessed are you poor, for yours is the kingdom of God."

These are the Beatitudes. But I wanted to know what that word meant, so after reading them in my Bible *(hold up Bible)*, I looked up the word *beatitude* in my dictionary *(hold up dictionary)*. See why Christians need a strong education? It comes in handy for understanding and talking about God's world! Well, *beatitude* means "the highest form of heavenly happiness, supreme blessedness; blessings spoken in regard to particular virtues." *Beatitude* comes from a Latin word that means "happy."

132

So then I got to thinking. What does blessing mean? What do you think it means? *(Pause.)* I thought blessings had to come from God. But the Bible says *we* can give blessings *to* God. So what are blessings? *(Pause.)* The dictionary says blessings make us happy, glorify us, give us heavenly joy. Those are things we want for those we love, for ourselves—and for our heavenly Father, right?

Have any of you mourned, that is, been very sad, because someone died? *(Pause.)* Have you ever cried? Have you ever been hated just because you love Jesus? Because you talked about him? *(Pause.)* These are tough things—things Jesus knows about because they happened to him too.

When Jesus told his friends about the Beatitudes, he promised that the sad, those hated because they loved Jesus, and the poor will be blessed with many things. And remember, blessings are the best kind of heavenly happiness. Wow!

So when you're sad, broken, hated, and crying, try to remember this: Your Father knows. Jesus knows. They've even been there! And they know just what *you* need and are glad to give it to you. They give you their very, very best, don't they?

Let's pray. *(Ask a child to pray or use the following.)* Father, the Bible can be filled with big words. Help me take the time to pray about them, look them up, and ask about them. Help me to remember that learning more about you brings many, many blessings. Thanks for that too! Amen.

The Grim Reaper

The Point of It All

Paul said we will reap what we sow. Therefore, we might want to take a close look at what we're spreading!

Objects

Two packets of seeds, or two small apple tree seedlings, or apple seeds from fruit you've eaten during the week (separated into two piles)

To Dos

Pray, rest, relax. Think about the seeds you sow. Think about your love walk, ministry, work, and kindness. But also reflect on your anger in traffic, impatience with your children, or other areas in which you may need work. Is there any way to improve your consistency? We're all human, but one stray seed can grow quite a weed!

Verse to Pray On

Galatians 6:7

Do not be deceived, God is not mocked; for whatever a man sows, that he will also reap.

Ready, Set, Go!

(Welcome kids, nod, wink, and so on to make each one feel special.) Good to see you! Ready for a story? OK!

Not long ago, not far away, there was a good man who was a farmer. He gave jobs to the nearby college kids and sold only the prettiest, freshest fruits and vegetables to the parents in the town. Those parents loved the farmer because his delicious crops actually made the kids want to eat vegetables. Can you believe that? *(Pause and smile.)*

Well, that farmer's best crop was apples. They were so delicious, kids would even stop by his farm to buy them.

Most of the kids bought red apples, but a few really, really liked his golden apples. Mmm! Year after year it was the same. And year after year everyone was happy.

Well, one year a storm came and really messed things up. That poor farmer lost many of his crops—even his precious apple trees. So he had nothing left to do but replant—and wait for those trees to grow. Since most of the kids loved red apples, he planted mostly those kinds of trees. Then he planted just a few trees for the kids who loved the beautiful, golden apples. *(Hold up your saplings or seeds as you speak.)* He planned and he planted. He did everything perfectly—or so the good farmer thought.

Years passed. And more years passed! Finally, the fruit showed up on those beautiful apple trees. But instead of fields and fields of bright red apple trees topped off with a crown of golden yellow apple trees—it was just the reverse!

There had been a mix-up. The good farmer had been so upset by the storm and its mess that he had planted the wrong trees. All those years wasted! Now, that farmer could have gone out there and done any number of things, but it wouldn't have changed the color of those apples. And it wouldn't have changed what the kids needed either. No amount of wishing or hoping or fussing would change the red apples to gold or the gold apples to red. For he reaped what he sowed. He got what he planted!

And that's the way it is for us. If we sow seeds of good things, like kindness and love, forgiveness and joy, we'll get those things back. Those are the things we will reap—or receive. Even in bad times we have to pay attention. Maybe *especially* in bad times we have to watch what we plant.

If we plant the wrong things—ugly words, mean looks, fits of temper—that's what we'll get back. Even if we don't mean to throw that fit or say that ugly word. Even if times are rough. We need to slow down and watch what we're planting, because the problems we cause could last many,

many years. And nothing we do can change that—except to be careful in the first place.

What are we going to plant today? We might want to double-check!

Let's pray. *(Ask a child to pray or use the following.)* Father, help me to keep checking my crop. Am I planting kindness? Am I trying to be loving and patient and gentle—even to those who make that hard? Please help me. I want to be like you, Father. Amen.

The Long Road Home

The Point of It All

Moses took many detours on the road to the Promised Land. Is fear getting in the way on our trip home? Are some detours a good idea?

Objects

Large, hand-drawn map including landmarks in the area surrounding your church (Use stick people, stick houses, etc. Go for cute, not accurate.)
Bible

To Dos

Spend time in prayer. Is there a route you're avoiding, or are you on track? Finding God's time and not rushing, yet not dallying, can be a prayerful pursuit.

Verse to Pray On

Deuteronomy 30:4

If any of you are driven out to the farthest parts under heaven, from there the LORD your God will gather you, and from there He will bring you.

Ready, Set, Go!

Good to see you! How many of you came to church today? *(Pause.)* Everyone! Excellent! How many of you drove? *(Pause.)* Nobody? Oh. Well, who drove you? *(Pause.)* Ah! How many of you drove the long way to get here? How many of you went to the library and the post office first? *(Name landmarks the kids will understand are out of the way.)* Did anybody make a stop on the way here? *(Pause.)*

Most of the time I take the shortest route to church on Sunday mornings. *(Use your map as you talk.)* Unless I've promised to pick up a friend or need to make a quick stop at the store, I take the shortest way here. Same for you? *(Pause.)* But what if I drove to the post office without stopping—it's closed on Sundays—and then drove to the library without stopping—just to see it—and then drove five more miles out of my way and then came to church? Maybe I'm nervous about doing the children's message, so I just drive around and around. What would happen? *(Pause.)*

I must admit, sometimes I do put off what I need to do. Cleaning my room. Putting away my clothes. Doing my homework—bills and stuff. I'm never sure why. Sometimes it's hard. Sometimes I think I'm too busy and just won't make time. Sometimes I'm afraid I won't get it right. Do you ever put off doing things you need to do? *(Pause.)*

Then you know that taking the long way around doesn't work so well. Sometimes it's OK. Sometimes it's even helpful—like if I don't clean my room so I can help my mom

137

in her garden or something like that. But sometimes putting off doing things really goofs me up—like it did Moses when he and the Israelites wandered around in the desert for forty years. *(Hold up Bible.)* Forty years!

I figure if that could happen to a smart guy like Moses, I could get lost sometimes too. Sometimes it's a good idea to stop and ask for directions. *(Smile wickedly at the women in the pews!) Some* people don't like to do that. But sometimes it makes sense. How can I get directions from God? How can I ask him where I should go and when? *(Pause.)*

That's right! I can read the Bible. I can pray. I can check things out with other Christians. After all, if I just keep going in the wrong direction without stopping, I might get lost in the desert. And even forty minutes is a long time to be lost in that heat!

Let's pray. *(Ask a child to pray or use the following.)* Father, you know our hearts. You know what you've called us to do. Help us to stop and ask for directions. Are we going the right way? Are we on the right track? Help us to follow you. Amen.

This Little Light of Mine

The Point of It All

Do we keep our light under a bushel? Do we use our gifts?

Objects

Flashlights, as many as you can gather

Lined, woven handbag or basket; must retain most of the light

To Dos

Test flashlights/batteries.

Get accomplices in the pews and give them flashlights.

Ask the pianist to be ready to play "This Little Light of Mine."

Arrange for someone to turn out the lights just before your sermon.

Read Matthew 5:1–16 aloud to yourself. Journal about what you find. Do you have a light in *your* bushel basket?

Verses to Pray On

Matthew 5:14–16

You are the light of the world. A city that is set on a hill cannot be hidden. Nor do they light a lamp and put it under a basket, but on a lampstand, and it gives light to all who are in the house. Let your light so shine before men, that they may see your good works and glorify your Father in heaven.

Ready, Set, Go!

(Bring your large handbag or basket to the front. Ask that all the lights be turned out. Total darkness is not necessary, just enough that flashlights will shine on the ceiling.)

The world can sometimes be a dark place, just like our church now. See that light over there? *(Point to a light left on in another part of the sanctuary.)* That's another Christian shining in the dark. You can be like her. *(Tell the kids what you have in the bag; show them the dark bag and dark flashlights. Then reach in, turn them all on, and close the bag, letting little light escape.)*

How much good do these lights do anybody? *(Pause. Slowly pull the flashlights out of the bag, giving one to as many children as you can.)* Here is your light. Let it shine. Point it at the ceiling *(do the same)* and make it dance like mine. Mine alone isn't very strong, but add yours and yours. See? *(At this point, those in the pews should add their lights. Just enjoy the "light show" for a bit.)*

You know what? I think I feel a song in my heart. Here it comes! *(Cue pianist.)* Remember "This Little Light of Mine"? Let's all sing it. That will be our prayer today—that we *all* let our lights shine. Please Lord, help us hear the words as we sing. Let us commit to them. Amen.

Let's sing! *(You may want to excuse the children as they sing. Cue the lights back on when all is finished and quietly return to your seat.)*

Walking the Plank

The Point of It All

Jesus said not to judge others or we'll be judged. If we take care of our own faults first, we'll be busy for a lifetime!

Objects

One leg of pantyhose (cut off from a pair)
One large foam tube, such as pipe insulation or a "pool noodle"

To Dos

Tie leg of pantyhose around the foam tube.

Wrap hose around your head bandana style. Knot in back so foam tube bobs wildly, looking as though it's sticking out from your eye.

Get an accomplice to have a "speck" in his or her eye.

Pray about why we tend to focus on the faults of others. I often find myself wondering why others are so critical! Why do I always want to fix someone else's wagon when my own often runs on three wobbly wheels?

Verses to Pray On

Matthew 7:3, 5

And why do you look at the speck in your brother's eye, but do not consider the plank in your own eye? . . . First remove the plank from your own eye, and then you will see clearly to remove the speck from your brother's eye.

Ready, Set, Go!

(Bounce head back and forth to exaggerate presence of "plank," but act as if you can't imagine why your audience is laughing.)

What? What? *What?* *(Ignoring the "plank" in your eye, walk up to one of the kids and try to get the "speck" out of his eye. Let him know beforehand so he can pretend he has dust in his eye. Be elaborate. Keep bumping into him with the piece of foam.)*

Hey! Let me help you. You've got something in your eye. *(Ad-lib as you go. Show surprise and earnest misunderstanding. As things wind down, discuss how silly you looked. Ask the kids the first thing they noticed.)*

141

That's right. So who *really* had a problem? Yeah, and everybody knew it, didn't they? Christ says not to judge or we'll be judged—or criticized. You know, we shouldn't gossip, pick on people, or think we know better all the time.

OK, what did Jesus say to do? "First remove the plank from your own eye." *(Do this with great finesse and a sigh of relief.)*

Ah, now I can see. Wow! And now I can see clearly to remove the speck of dust from my brother's eye! *(Remove speck and hold it out for all to see. Of course, there isn't one to see!)* There, see it? Big, isn't it? Wow! How did he live with that big old telephone pole of a plank in his eye? *(Pause.)* What?

You don't see it? Really? *(Pause.)* You know what, you're right. It's so easy to focus on others' faults until they seem like *telephone poles!* But we can't even see straight because we have telephone poles in our own eyes—big problems *we* need to solve. After all, Jesus was the only perfect one. If we were perfect, we'd be loving those with specks in their eyes, not trying to beat them to death with the poles in our own eyes, right? You are *so* smart!

Let's pray. *(Ask a child to pray or use the following.)* Father, you know we try to do our best but still make many mistakes. Sometimes those mistakes hurt others. Please help us to be kind first, as you have asked. Help us to love, not criticize, those around us—no matter how often we feel upset. Amen.

Pretty Petty Patty

The Point of It All

We often want what other people have—and sometimes we're not even sure what that is!

Objects

Candy or pastry (wrapped)
Hot chocolate mug/packet of hot chocolate
Pretty gift bag or box
Remote control

To Dos

Think and pray about what you want. Think about the last time you envied someone else. Could there be headaches attached you don't know about? Are you sure you want them? Why doesn't God want us to covet?

Verses to Pray On

Exodus 20:17

You shall not covet your neighbor's house; you shall not covet your neighbor's wife, nor his male servant, nor his female servant, nor his ox, nor his donkey, nor anything that is your neighbor's.

Psalm 56:3–4

Whenever I am afraid,
I will trust in You.
In God (I will praise His word),
In God I have put my trust;
I will not fear.
What can flesh do to me?

Ready, Set, Go!

Today I'm going to tell you a story.

143

In a small town, not so long ago, there lived a bunch of sweet Christian kids. Now, most of these kids—Mary and her friends—took the bus to school each morning. And as they passed a very pretty house, they saw a very pretty girl through its very pretty windows. They called her Pretty Petty Patty because she never had to go to school or do any work. Petty Patty got to stay home and have breakfast served to her on a beautiful tray by her beautiful mom. She drank (they were sure) the best hot chocolate out of the fanciest mugs. *(Hold up mug.)* Petty Patty passed the day in the most wonderful ways. She wore beautiful clothes without spot or wrinkle. And the kids were sure she had the best toys. And as they passed her each day on their way to school and tests, sit-ups and teachers, they nearly hated her tiny feet that were propped on a silken pillow.

Through Petty Patty's picture-perfect window, Mary and friends could see the TV. They were sure she sat all day watching the best cartoons. *(Hold up remote control.)* They saw that she had many visitors and received many gifts. *(Hold up gift bag.)* Everybody wanted to be Petty Patty— don't you? *(Pause.)*

That's what all the kids thought. Sometimes they even noticed Petty Patty's fluffy white kitten curled up on her shoulder as Petty Patty read books or ate off her beautiful dishes. They were sure that the trays Petty Patty's mom delivered were piled high with cakes and candies. *(Hold up your pastry.)* Mmm! Delicious pies and even—they were sure—cheeseburgers!

And no school!

Finally, Mary stood up on that bus and shouted: "I can't take it anymore. I hate school! I love TV! We deserve cakes and candies. We deserve to relax. I need a kitten curled about my neck as I watch the bus drive by. I bet that girl laughs at us each time we go to school!"

Now, Mary had a plan. She told her friends what they should do. They should visit Petty Patty and pretend they wanted to get to know her. They remembered a time when

Pretty Petty Patty (just Patty then) had played outdoors with them—back before she turned into a TV-watching, sweet-eating snob!

"We'll knock on her door," Mary continued, "and we'll ask to come in. I'm sure she will let us play with her toys and eat her cakes. We should have those treats too!"

So the next day the girls got off the bus and walked the short distance to Petty Patty's house. They knocked on the door. Patty's mom welcomed them in.

However, on this side of the picture-perfect window, they saw a different sight. Petty Patty's hair was thin and lifeless. Her face was stretched and sickly. Her lovely tan of summers ago was gone. And although Petty Patty smiled with polite surprise at Mary and her friends, she did not smile wide. She smiled weakly, for she was sick, very sick. She could barely move, in fact.

Petty Patty's mom spoke fast and walked faster. She too was thin and weak in an exhausted, worried way. She was nearly see-through pale!

"I'm so glad you girls stopped by," Patty's mom squeaked. "My sweet, pretty Patty has missed you all these years. Let me get us something to eat."

Patty's mom pulled out her finest china tea set. "For such a special occasion," she explained to Mary and her friends. Then she pulled out the cakes and candies. She placed that special tray on Patty's lap. Petty Patty did not move. She was too weak to move from the sunny window, just as she had been on all those other days when they had envied her.

"I love to bake," Patty's mom said. "It makes the house smell so wonderful. Just like old times! Now if I could just coax my pretty Patty to eat a bit of these treats. Maybe you could set a good example by nibbling on my chocolate chip cookies!"

But suddenly Mary and her friends had lost their appetite for Patty's life.

By the time the girls left, they had promised to return tomorrow. Patty had been carried off to lie down, as one of her headaches had tired her so.

Do you think Mary and her friends still want to be Petty Patty? *(Pause.)* You're right. Now they understand why Patty has the gifts—the sweets and treats. They understand why Patty is so thin and her clothes so neat and pretty. Why she doesn't go to school.

Now, riding the bus to school with all of their friends just isn't that bad, they say.

And today, each time they pass Pretty Patty's picture-perfect window, they wave and smile. And they mean it. And they still visit and share the blessings that are Pretty Patty's—love, understanding, and strength.

Let's pray. *(Ask a child to pray or use the following.)* Father, we judge our insides by other people's outsides. We judge ourselves and our lives by what we *think* we see. Help us to reach out in love and find the gift of true peace and happiness. Help us to trust that what you give us is *exactly* what we need to be happy. Amen.

Live the Golden Rule— Mean Kids Drool!

The Point of It All

Telling the truth: When is it a good idea? When is it gossip—or just plain cruel? How do we know?

Objects

Bob the Puppet dressed in something ugly—maybe with an ugly hat

146

An ugly outfit (shoes, hat, etc.)
something Bob can insult

To Dos

Practice with Bob.

Ask God for guidance. Wha...
ful? What is a lie? What is biblica...
Do you remember a time when you told an un...
essary "truth" and injured another? Was a child ever
brutally honest with you? How did you feel afterward? Does that "truth" still hurt when you remember it today?

Verses to Pray On

John 8:32

*You shall know the truth, and the truth shall make you
free.*

1 John 3:11

*For this is the message that you heard from the begin-
ning, that we should love one another.*

Ready, Set, Go!

Hello! Guess who I brought with me today? He wanted
to visit. *(Pause.)* That's right—Bob! We've been working
with him. I'm really praying that his manners are improv-
ing. If not, though, maybe you can help me guide him a
little closer to, well, uh, manners. Lately Bob and I have
been working on telling the truth.

eah, and, to tell the truth, I *honestly* think it all stinks! I mean, truth depends on whom you talk to.

You: Bob, not now.

Bob: *Honestly*, I think we need to talk about it now! It's like that window I broke. My friends said I broke it. I say they broke it. It *honestly* depends on whom you ask.

You: Bob, I saw you hit the homerun. You never slowed down as you ran the bases. You cheered when your ball smashed Mrs. Smith's window. It was you. That's the truth!

Bob: Well, that's *one* version of the story. Depends on whom you ask. I see it differently. Like that tie (dress, hat) you're wearing. I *honestly* think it is the *ugliest* thing I've ever seen. Now I guess, since you paid good money for it, chose it, and wore it today, you like it. Depends on whom you ask. But *honestly*, it's ugleeee! Just thought you'd like to know. It's the truth.

You: Bob! How rude.

Bob: Just telling the truth. The truth will set you free! It's right in the Bible. In fact, Jesus said it. I can show it to you. That's the truth.

You: You know, you may be right. But maybe not. I like my tie (dress, hat). It's, well, different! But you hurt my feelings, Bob. And you embarrassed me. You know, God wants us to love one another, to treat one another like we'd like to be treated. That's the most important thing. You know, live the Golden Rule—mean kids drool!

Bob: Well, I *honestly* don't *love* your *tie*. I love you. Not the tie.

You: OK. So how do we know what truths need to be told? If I think you look bad in something or don't like your outfit, do I need to tell you? You know, like you just told me?

Bob: What's not to like? No, don't tell me.

You: How about if I *think* something's true, like a bit of gossip? Should I tell?

Bob: What did you hear? *(Quick. With a snap of the head in your direction, then the kids' faces, then yours again.)*

You: The answer, Bob, is no. It's not OK to pass on gossip! Not unless someone is in danger. In fact, I was given a three-question list I use to find out whether or not to tell something.

(Say them slowly. Count on your fingers as you go.) (1) Is it kind? (2) Is it true? (3) Is it necessary? At least two of the answers need to be yes to tell. Take my tie, for instance—not kind, not necessary. Don't say it!

Gossip. Not kind. Not necessary. Probably not even true! Same goes, uh, excuse me, for your outfit.

Bob: What? What are you trying to tell me?

You: Nothing, Bob. It's not kind or necessary! Anyway, the guiding rule is the Golden Rule. We need to treat others like we want to be treated. I don't like to be hurt or embarrassed. I truly hate gossip and rumors. And I don't want to do that to somebody else. So I live the Golden Rule and remember that at least two must be true: Is it kind? Is it true? Is it necessary?

If two out of three aren't true, it probably isn't a loving thing to do. And love *must* come first. The rest really *does* depend on whom you ask—at least sometimes. *Hey,* Bob, how about that window? I need to get that money from you to replace the window!

Bob: Uh, gotta go! And that's the *truth! (Slip him under your arm.)*

Let's pray. *(Ask a child to pray or use the following.)* Father, make sure we know the truth before we speak it. Help us to be kind and loving and to always put your people first. Amen.

God's Got Your Back!

The Point of It All

God is right behind me, whether I can see him or not.

Objects

Dog leash (if you use a dog story), or a prop that represents a loss

To Dos

Warn your soon-to-be-exiled kids (see lesson).

Rest and pray about your tough times. When did you feel loneliest as a child? When did that change? How do you cure loneliness today?

Verse to Pray On

Matthew 28:20

I am with you always, even to the end of the age.

Ready, Set, Go!

Hi! Oh, it's good to see you. I see you, Heather. *(Point at, and name, several kids.)* I see you, Mary. Can you see me? It's so good to see each other. Hugs are great too. Do your parents give you hugs? Give a friend a hug, or pat him or her on the shoulder. Hugs make you feel like you can do anything, don't they?

Our "Big Parent," our heavenly Father, gives us hugs sometimes too. We watch a miracle happen in someone's life, or God just reaches down and pats us on the arm with an encouraging word. Maybe he sends a special friend or family member to give us a hug or say just the right thing at the right time.

Now move far away from one another. *(Exile a couple of kids to the far corners of the church. Maybe even send one outside—but warn them before the sermon. You don't want them to really feel this!)*

How does it feel? Lonely? Sometimes when I'm troubled or life is tough, I feel like God is far away—like last year when my dog Joey died. *(Give some such example; maybe you failed a school test or lost your way to a party. Use something they can understand.)* I couldn't understand why that would happen to me! Where was God?

But then I got to thinking. If my parents had always held me, given me everything I ever reached for, I never would have learned to walk. I'm sure I was scared as I toddled around the coffee table. I didn't realize they stood behind me in case I needed them. But they let me grow strong by walking on my own. I'm here today walking just fine. My head's not cracked open, so my parents must have done a good job!

As I've grown older, God has sometimes sent my parents, a friend, or aunt to hold my hand, visit me, or hug me. They seem to be God's earthly angels—sent to take care of me when I stumble or get hurt. They are, like a friend of mine says, "God with skin on." I can reach out and touch them, hold them, and know that God is nearby. Then I can find a quiet place and pray. By then I'm *sure* he's there.

Let's pray. *(Ask a child to pray or use the following.)* Father, remind me to comfort others. Remind me that when I'm scared and lonely you're right beside me. Amen.

Fill in the Blank

The Point of It All

Rain falls on us all. When trouble comes, it just means we're one of the gang. Many are the troubles of the righteous.

Objects

Squirt gun to make it "rain" on the "just"
Umbrella

To Dos

Pray about the verses. Do you ever wonder if you "deserve trouble"? Do you ever wonder if God is punishing you, or someone else, with hard times? Journal and tuck your writing into your Bible. Next time tragedy strikes, pull it out to remember that ours is a God of love.

Verses to Pray On

Psalm 34:19

*Many are the afflictions of the righteous,
But the LORD delivers him out of them all.*

Proverbs 24:16

*For a righteous man may fall seven times
And rise again,
But the wicked shall fall by calamity.*

Ready, Set, Go!

Today we're going to have a pop quiz. I'll say part of a quote and you fill in the blank. OK?

Jesus loves the little _____. *(Let them fill in the blank.)* Children! Good!

Noah built an _____. Ark! Great! God is _____. Love! Yes! OK, here's a hard one. Many are the troubles of the _____. *(Big pause. Expect your eyes to pop with the answers even adults will give!)* Righteous!

Yes, the righteous. The ones doing right. That means you can be doing your very best and troubles will still come. The rain falls on everybody. *(Squirt a few kids who won't mind.)* And trouble comes to everybody, good and bad. *(Squirt, squirt.)*

So is God picking on us? *(Squirt, squirt.)* I don't think so. He assures us that we're all in it together.

Look what Jesus went through. We'll never have it that hard. Never. And that pain is long gone for him now, just like it will be for the good people who suffer today. Heaven fixes everything. No more tears. It's a promise!

The point? We're gonna have troubles. We're gonna get sick, lose things, get shots, and have tons of homework— even worse sometimes.

Next time you ask, "Why me?" there may be a very good answer. . . . Many are the troubles of the _____ *(all together now)* righteous. And we'll help each other through, won't we? With God behind us all the way!

Yeah! *(Squirt, squirt.)* Oh, and an umbrella doesn't hurt either!

Let's pray. *(Ask a child to pray or use the following.)* Father, life can be tough. Sometimes I feel like I can't find the answers. But I know you understand rejection and loss, hardship and troubles. Please comfort me and send support for the hard times. I know you will. In Christ's name we pray. Amen.

Sword, Paper, Stones

The Point of It All

We all know much about the Bible. Have we confused any of it? We need to check our beliefs against God's Bible on a regular basis.

Objects

Smooth stone

Long piece of cloth that can fake a sling shot (just fold material in a U-shape like a soft belt and put your stone in it)

Rubber sword

Find something in your church that is over nine feet tall and can easily be seen by all. Cut a large face from paper, or use a ski mask to represent Goliath. Attach it at the top of the nine-foot-tall object near where you'll be teaching. A place where a boy can also stand for comparison would be best. Or even more effective, represent Goliath yourself and teach from a ladder, table, or pair of stilts that makes you more than nine feet tall. Bulk up under your outfit with balloons or toilet paper for muscles. If a muscle falls out or you wobble on your ladder, just roar, "What are you laughing at?"

To Dos

Write three things you think happened in the story of Goliath. Where did you hear them?

Read the story in 1 Samuel 17:9–54. Did Goliath die by a stone or a sword? Whose?

Gather above. Hang the nine-foot comparison object and arrange for a boy to stand near it on cue. Or organize your Goliath outfit. You could even have a volunteer play Goliath. Without scaring the children to death, you want them to realize what they would have felt like facing Goliath.

Read the entire story in the Bible. Close your eyes tight. Live the entire story: smell, hear, taste, feel it. Hear Goliath's frightening roar. Feel the threat of enslavement for your family. See the soldiers you've admired cower around you. Now take your smooth stones, say your prayers, and take on Goliath. Whew! It's a scary thing, isn't it? Now can you see those once intimidating Philistines flee before you? Can you feel Goliath's hairy, severed head in your hands? It's disgusting! Can you see King Saul as you present the head to him? The kids will love this story if you help them live it.

Verses to Pray On

The story of David and Goliath: 1 Samuel 17, especially verses 50–51:

> *So David prevailed over the Philistine with a sling and a stone, and struck the Philistine and killed him. But there was no sword in the hand of David. Therefore David ran and stood over the Philistine, took his sword and drew it out of its sheath and killed him, and cut off his head with it. And when the Philistines saw that their champion was dead, they fled.*

Ready, Set, Go!

Notice anything different today? *(Point out whatever represents Goliath.)* Amazing, huh? You all know the story of David and Goliath? Did you know Goliath was more than nine feet tall? Just like that! *(Point again.)* David was much smaller—just a harp-playing, youngest brother. Everybody thought David was too small to fight in a war. *Everybody* felt too small to fight nine-foot-tall Goliath!

Now, somebody tell me—quickly—the story of David and Goliath. *(Pause and encourage someone to tell. Correct anything they get wrong, except for the ending. If no one will talk, tell the story yourself and stop after Goliath's rock-to-the-head incident. Hold up your objects as you go.)*

Yes, yes, yes! Who says the Bible isn't exciting? You're not going to believe this, though. I thought that was the end of the story. *(If you knew better, say, "A friend of mine thought . . .")* I had heard the story so many times, I just figured I knew it all!

But what killed Goliath? *(Pause.)* The stone played a part, yes. But that's not all. Did David have a sword? No. But Goliath did. Do you know what happened next? *(Lean forward, hunch over, and speak in a slow, suspenseful voice.*

Let your eyes widen. This is an incredibly scary story you are about to tell.) Well! David—took—that—sword—right—from—Goliath's—sheath—its holder. *(Go slow, one word at a time. Act it out.)* David pulled out that great, big sword and killed Goliath. And cut off his head! *(Stop and bug out your eyes.)* Gross! It wasn't just a pebble that killed Goliath. It was his own sword!

And then *(pause and take a deep breath)—then!* Then David took that nasty old Goliath head to Jerusalem and carried it—by hand—to King Saul. Eew!

Now that's quite a lot *not* to know, isn't it? So I'm committed to checking it out, reading my Bible more today and always. And when someone tells me something, I want to read it for myself. There's a lot in this Bible! Some very smart people have spent their entire lives learning more and more about it. And it obviously has some pretty good stories in it. No tall tales these. This is real life!

Let's pray. *(Ask a child to pray or use the following.)* Father, you love a good story and tell the best. Help us to study this glorious history that is ours, that teaches us to be brave and to trust in you. Help us to remember what gifts and tales of suspense the Bible holds for all of us. And help us to share it with a friend, like my sweet friends here. Amen.

Subject Index

Scripture Index

Annette Godwin Dammer teaches writing at Fayetteville Tech Community College in North Carolina. She also manages *Teen Light* magazine (www.teenlight.org) and conducts writing and teen journalism workshops.

Lynn Fisher Atchly teaches English at Fayetteville Christian School. She worships at Tabor United Methodist Church in Cedar Creek, North Carolina, where she assists the pastor with children's sermons.

RAVE

2

ÍNDICE

RAVE: 5 ✛ ¿¡VIAJAR, VIAJAR!?

YO DIRÍA QUE YA TENDRÍAMOS QUE HABER LLEGADO AL CONTINENTE...

QUÉ RARO...

¡EH! ¡PLUE!

TENGO QUE ENCONTRAR RÁPIDO A ESE TAL MÚSICA PARA QUE REPARE LA ESPADA...

ZAS

World-MAP

¿NOS HABREMOS EQUIVOCADO DE DIRECCIÓN?

GROOOOOOO

PUUN.

4

ASÍ QUE ESTO ES UNA CIUDAD...

CRAAA

CRAAA

¿¡DE DÓNDE SALE TANTA GENTE!?

¡¡AH!!

¡ES LA ZONA COMERCIAL!

¡PLUE, BUSQUEMOS UN SITIO DONDE COMER!

PLIN

¿ESTÁS AHÍ?

¡¡EH, PLUE!! ¿¡DÓNDE ESTÁS!?

¡¡PLUE!!

7

NO PUEDE EVITARLO.

SIENTO QUE LE HAYA MOLESTADO...

JA, JA, JA...

MA... ¿MA-JO?

JA, JA...

VENGA, VAMOS.

¿HASTA CUÁNDO PIENSAS COMER?

SRISH

!

POM

¡GRACIAS, SEÑOR!

PÁGAME.

NO TAN RÁPIDO... ESE PERRO SE HA COMIDO 30 DE MIS DULCES...

RRR

GR

RRRRR

¡NO TENGO TANTO DINERO!

¿¡MEDIO MILLÓN!?

SON MEDIO MILLÓN DE EDELS.

SE-ÑOR...

EDEL (E)= ES LA MONEDA DE ESE PAÍS.

¿QUIERES COMPROBARLO? ¿LE EXAMINAMOS LA BARRIGA A ESE CHUCHO?

CALLA, NIÑATO... SE HA COMIDO TREINTA.

!!

¿¡TANTO DINERO SÓLO POR PIRU-LETAS!?

¡¡PLUE SÓLO SE HA COMIDO CINCO!!

PERO AUN ASÍ 5 SON UNA PASTA...

¿EH?

ZUMM

SI NO ME QUIERES PAGAR...

JEJE

A VER SI TE EXAMINO YO A TI...

GRMMM

...

¿¡QUÉ PIENSA HACER CON ÉL!?

FIIIEP

ME QUEDO CON EL PERRO.

RRRRRRRRRRRRR

¡KS!

RAZZR!

BLUE ERIS

¿¡PERO QUÉ PRE-TENDE!?

TAP TAP

¡DE-VUÉLVA-MELO!

BROOOOUM

¡ESPERE!

¿SE LLAMA PLUE?

BROOOOM

TIENES
RAZÓN.

¡TOCA EL
RELEVO!

NO
PUEDO
HACER
NADA
HASTA
MAÑA-
NA...

TAP

SI ESTU-
VIÉRAMOS
EN LA ISLA
GARAGE YA
LO HUBIERA
ENCON-
TRADO...

ESTE
CONTI-
NENTE
ES
ENOR-
ME.

ARF
ARF

ARF.

ARF.

12

¿PERROS?

¡POR SUPUESTO, SEÑOR!

JO... A BUSCAR ALGO A MEDIA JORNADA...

¡OS COSTARÁ EL SUELDO DE ESTE MES!

¿NO PODÉIS ENCARGAROS NI DE UN CRÍO?

BAH... NO ERES MÁS QUE UN PATÉTICO SUBORDINADO.

¡¡NO HAY DUDA!! ¡ES ESE CHICO!

!

ESTE CHICO ME RESULTA FAMILIAR...

ESTE CRÍO... ¡TIENE UNA FUERZA SOBRE HUMANA!

YA ESTÁ BIEN, JOVENCITO.

¡UAHHH!!

MEJOR
DICHO...
SUCESOR
DE RAVE.

CHAN

CHAN

DEMON CARD:

GEORCO

¡¡ES DE
DEMON
CARD!!

ZRISH

ESE
SÍMBOLO...

RAVE: 6 ✚ VIVO O MUERTO

NO SÉ DE QUÉ TE EXTRAÑAS SI VIENES A LA CENTRAL DE DEMON CARD DE ESTA ZONA.

SUCESOR.

¡SÓLO QUIERO QUE ME DEVOLVÁIS A PLUE!

NO ME IMPORTA QUE SEAS DE DEMON CARD, NI QUE SEAS UN MAFIOSO U ORGANICES CARRERAS DE PERROS.

OO OOO

¿ASÍ QUE ESE PERRO ES TUYO?

BUENO... NO SÉ SI ES UN PERRO.

UUAAH

EL PERRO QUE NO CORRIO.

TAP TAP

¿PLUE?

CRICK

UUAAH

UUAAH

NO PODEMOS DÁRTELO.

SNAPP

OOO

OOOO

PERO ES QUE NOSOTROS LO HEMOS COMPRADO.

COMPRENDO...

¡PROVOCARÉ UNA EXPLOSIÓN!

¡¡PUEDE QUE NO TENGA ESPADA, PERO TENGO A RAVE!!

¡ALLÁ VOY!

ESE TIPO... LES VENDIÓ A PLUE...

GÑNNNÑ

SLASH!

UUUO FF

GRRR

JU.

ii...!!

TE DUELE, ¿VERDAD?

COF

COF

NINGUNO DE SUS ATAQUES SERÁ EFECTIVO A CAUSA DEL HUMO.

ES IMPOSIBLE.

FIUU

ZAS

NO LE HE DADO.

SI LE GOLPEO EN LA CARA...

¡¡ESO ES!! ¡¡SU CARA!!

TENGO QUE HUIR CON PLUE...

¿PERO CO- MO?

JU, JU, JU...

FUASH

COF

¡¡SÍ!!

¿¡QUÉ HACÉIS!? ¡BUSCADLO INMEDIATAMEN- TE! ¡O PERDERÉ MI PROMO- CIÓN!

FSSSSSH

TSK... ¿HA DESA- PARE- CIDO?

ESE CHICO HA HUIDO...

!

HAZ QUE ESE PERRO PARTICIPE EN LA SIGUIENTE CARRERA.

ESPERA... SE ME HA OCURRIDO ALGO DIVERTIDO...

¿EH?

¡ESTE PERRO NO PUEDE ENTRAR EN LA SIGUIEN- TE CARRE- RA, ES MUY SANGRIEN- TA!

¡¡...!!

LO QUE QUIERO ES QUE EL CHICO SALGA...

NO ME IMPORTA.

ARF.

ARF.

DEBE DE ESTAR POR AQUÍ, ¡BUSCADLO!

¡SIENTO LA INTERRUPCIÓN!

ZACK

HRA

ZAS

?

TUTUM

UAAAH

UAAAH

¿HA VISTO A ESE CHICO TAN RARO?

HRA

AAAH

UAAAH

...

QUÉ VA.

¿ii...!!?

ZACK

¿CÓ-MO!? ¿NO SE-RÁ QUE QUIERES VERME LA ROPA INTE-RIOR!?

YO LA VEO...

...

¿PUEDO VER LO QUE TIENE DEBAJO DE LA SILLA?

...

¡BUSQUE-MOS POR ALLÍ!

¡SÍ!

HUBCH

TAP TAP TAP

¿ELIE?

¡EH, TÚ! ¡ELIE NO TIENE NADA QUE VER!

TAP TAP TAP

UAAAH

ZAS

UAAAH

UAAAH

UAAAH

FRAS

UAAAH

...

¿HABLAS DE DEMON CARD?

ESTABAN MUY ENFADADOS.

DE NADA.

JE JE

EH... GRACIAS.

¿EH? ¿NO ERES DE ESTA CIUDAD?

SÍ. ESTA CIUDAD, COMO MUCHAS OTRAS, ESTÁ BAJO SU CONTROL.

¿Y QUÉ HAS VENIDO A HACER AQUÍ?

QUÉ VA, VENGO DE LA ISLA GARAGE.

ENCANTADO.

¿DE VERAS?

35

AH.....

PUES... LA VERDAD ES QUE ESTOY EN MEDIO DE UN VIAJE...

¿LEYES?

¿LO SABES, HARU? EN ESTA CIUDAD CONTROLA-DA POR DEMON CARD HAY LEYES MUY ESTRICTAS.

IGUAL QUE YO.

FLIPO

CLA-RO.

¿EH!?

¿DE VER-DAD!? ¿YO TAM-BIÉN?

A DEMON CARD.

NO HAY PROBLEMAS PARA ENTRAR EN LA CIU-DAD, PERO TIENES QUE PAGAR MUCHO DINERO PARA PODER SALIR...

PA-RECE QUE NOS PERSI-GUEN LOS PRO-BLE-MAS...

JO... DESDE QUE TENGO A PLUE...

BONK

BA-FF

EN CUANTO ACABE LA CARRERA.

YO ME MARCHO HOY. ♡

CUANDO ACABE LA CARRERA TE DIRÉ CÓMO.

NO... GRACIAS, PERO... NO TENGO ESE DINERO.

JE JE

PAGAREMOS EL DINERO DE LA TASA Y SALDREMOS JUNTOS DE LA CIUDAD.

¿CÓMO PUEDO RECUPERAR A PLUE?

DEPRE

JO... NO ESTOY DE HUMOR PARA VER CARRERAS...

¡ESTÁ A PUNTO DE EMPEZAR LA CARRERA PRINCIPAL DE HOY, LA BATTLE ROAD!

GUAU GUAU

ARF ARF

¿...?

¡¡YA EMPIEZA!!

Y ENTONCES, COMO PARTE DE DEMON CARD...

HARÉ QUE TODOS VEAN MI TERRIBLE SMOKE BAR.

ZU MM

UAAAH UAAAH UAAAH UAH

LO SIENTO, DEBO DETENER LA CARRERA.

ELIE.

TAP

¡TENGO QUE AYUDAR A PLUE!

¿ii EH !!?

¿PLUE ES TU PERRO?

BA MM

CLA SP TAP

PATAM

¡¡ESTÁ CASI VOLANDO!!

MIRA.

ZUMM

¡SEGURO QUE AL FINAL SALE VOLANDO!

YO... ¿¡¡VOLANDO!!?

EH... DICES QUE ES UN BICHO... ¿Y ENTONCES CÓMO VA A GANAR?

ESTA CHICA...

Y VENDRÁ EL TIPO DE ANTES...

OO OOO

BAMM

¡NINGÚN PERRO HA MUERTO EN LA BATTLE ROAD!

¡SI QUIERES INTERVENIR EN LA CARRERA, SÓLO HAS DE APRETAR ESTE BOTÓN!

DOMM

SI SIGUE ASÍ, PLUE...

BLIN

PATAM

¡¡PLUE!!

RAVE: 7 ✚ LA VENGANZA DEL TRÍO.

BUUU BUUU BUUU

Y A CONTINUACIÓN...

¡SI MUERE ALGUNO DE LOS PERROS LAS APUESTAS NO SE DEVUELVEN!

IMPOSIBLE...

...

...

JAMÁS... HABÍA VISTO UNA CARRERA COMO ÉSTA.

NO ES... LA BATTLE ROAD DE SIEMPRE.

FIUU FIUU FIUU

¡HAN ENTRADO EN LA ZONA DE LAS PICAS!

CHAC CHAC CHAC CHAC

¡SE RETIRAN OTROS DOS PERROS!

NO AGUANTO MÁS.

¿DÓN-DE?

¡SEÑOR GEORCO! ¡LO HEMOS ENCON-TRADO!

GATE 16 ... NORMAL

PIII

¡PREPA-RADLO TODO!

¡ADE-LANTE!

BAFF

PIII

PIII

¡SE DIRIGE A LA ZONA DE CA-RRERAS POR LA PUERTA 16!

ACABEMOS DE UNA VEZ POR TODAS...

BLINC

Fight DOORCHAIN

BAM·MM ¡¡PLUE!!

¡NOS VAMOS AHORA MISMO DE AQUÍ!

PUUN

¡NO ME SALUDES!

TONTO

TIPI TIPI
BRR
BRR

BOUM BOUM BOUM

¡PLUE!

BOUM BOUM BOUM BOUM

¿QUÉ PERRO SERÁ LA VÍCTIMA DE LAS BOMBAS?

!

¡CO-MIENZA LA BOMBA PERSE-CUTORIA!

JU, JU, JU...

!!

OOOOOM

A MI SMOKE BAR.

BIENVE-NIDO...

ZU

MM

MIERDA, NO PODRÉ LEVANTAR-LO.

GRRR

NO TE ESFUERCES, PESA 4 TONELA-DAS.

¿¡QUÉ!?

ZRISH

¿SMO-KE BAR?

¡¡LA CÁMARA SECRETA!!

CONOCERÁS EL TERROR DEL HUMO...

¿¡QUÉ HAGO!?

CINCO MINUTOS... NO, UNOS DOS O TRES...

CREO QUE PODRÉ AGUANTAR...

VALE.

¡DEBO DERROTARLO EN ESE INTERVALO!

¡DEJARÉ DE RESPIRAR!

! CLONG

SI ROMPIERA LA PARED PODRÍA SALIR AL EXTERIOR...

Y, SIN OXÍGENO, NO HAY EXPLOSIONES.

EN ESTE ESPACIO NO HAY OXÍGENO.

NO...

NO HA EXPLOTADO...

PUUN

FRAS

FRASS

!?

JE, JE, JE...

CRICK

¡NO PODRÁS DETONAR NADA, ASÍ QUE NO TIENES ESCAPATORIA!

AAAH

NO...

AGUANTO MÁS...

PERRO IDIOTA.

¿QUIERES HACER UN AGUJERO PARA HUIR? NO TE DARÁ TIEMPO, ANTES MORIRÁS ASFIXIADO.

56

SUCESOR DE RAVE.

¿YA ESTÁ? ESPERABA ALGO MÁS DE TI...

¡VAMOS, MUERE!

FUOOO

IMPOSIBLE... NO TENGO FUERZAS...

CLOC

VOY A MORIR AQUÍ...

!?

PERO...
¿Y ESTA
EXPLO-
SIÓN!?

FSSHH
FSSHH

FIUU

¡¡UAAAH!!

?

FSSHH

¡HA
DESTRO-
ZADO MI
CÁMARA
SECRETA!

OOOOOH!

¡iC.O. HEYUN!!

¡NO PODRÁS HUIR!

JUA JUA JUA

...

PRONTO NO TEN-DRÁS QU... PREOCU... PARTE PO... ESTE ES... TÚPIDO CHUCHO

¿DÓN-DE SE HA ME-TIDO!?

¿DÓNDE ESTÁ MI DARK BRING!?

TUIN TUIN

...

!?

?

ES... ¡ESPERA! ¡HABLEMOS UN POCO! ¡SEGURO QUE PODEMOS ARREGLAR-LO!

SLASH

¡¡BIEN HECHO, PLUE!!

¡AHÍ ES-TÁ!

GLUPS

FRUUN

BRR

RAVE: 8 ✚ LA MAGIA DE LA SONRISA

PA TAM

JE.

¿¡QUÉ HACE-MOS!?

HA GOL-PEADO... AL SEÑOR GEORCO...

TAPP!

FLIP

EN ESE CASO... ¡¡HUYA-MOS!!

¡¡MÁS IDIO-TAS!!

TSK... ESA ELIE SIGUE DESTRO-ZÁNDOLO TODO...

¡ASÍ ESTÁ MEJOR, DESPEJADO!

FLIPO

CLONG

¡HEY!

JE

PERO ME HA AYUDADO...

QUÉ CHICA MÁS RARA, NO TIENE NADA QUE VER CON LO QUE DECÍA MI HERMANA QUE ERA UNA CHICA.

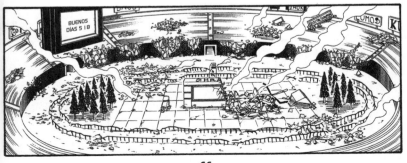

BUENOS DÍAS 518

¡POR CIERTO, HARU!

¿QUÉ DICES?

?

AL FIN Y AL CABO ME AYUDASTE.

PERO A MÍ ME GUSTA...

¡¡NI HABLAR!! ¡Y NO ES UN INSECTO!

¡DAME ESTE INSECTO PORFA!

ZRISH

PUUN

MIRA

BRR

TAP TAP TAP

BRR

¡AH!

wii wii

CREO QUE SERÁ UNA BUENA ALMOHADA.

¿ALMOHADA? ¿LO QUIERES DE COJÍN?

TIPI TIPI

?

CL

PUUN.

EEP

67

TAP TAP TAP

PUUN.

BRR BRR

GRRR

GRRR

GRRR

PUUN.

BRR BRR

PUES SÍ SERÁ UN PERRO...

MIRA, HA IDO A AYUDAR A SUS COMPAÑEROS...

EN REALIDAD... BUSCO A UN TIPO QUE SE LLAMA MÚSICA.

BUENOS DÍAS 5:18

EH, HARU, ¿ADÓNDE TE DIRIGES?

MÚSICA, ¿EH?

YO BUSCO A UNA PERSONA, NO A UNA COSA...

VAYA... YO TAMBIÉN ESTOY BUSCANDO ALGO.

¿¡LE CONOCES!?

¿VES? NO ES DIFÍCIL ENCONTRARLE.

EL HERRERO MÚSICA.

!

PUNK STREET

HIP HOP TOWN

GARAGE·I

N
S

SÍ... LA CIUDAD MÁS IMPORTANTE DE VENTA DE ARMAS.

¿PUNK STREET?

NO PERSONALMENTE, PERO OÍ HABLAR DE ÉL EN PUNK STREET.

UNA DE LAS CIUDADES MÁS POBLADAS Y CAÓTICAS DEL MUNDO.

ES EL LUGAR DONDE CRIMINALES Y GENTE HONRADA COMPRAN SUS ARMAS.

MÚSICA ESTARÁ ALLÍ...

PUNK STREET...

¡A PUNK STREET!

¡¡LLÉVA-ME, POR FAVOR!!

SÍ, YA HE ESTADO ALLÍ.

ELIE, ¿CONOCES PUNK STREET?

¡VAYAMOS JUNTOS! ¡Y ASÍ PODRÉ AYUDARTE A ENCONTRAR LO QUE BUSCAS!

70

FIOOOOOOOOOOU

GRACIAS.

¡NO DIGAS NADA! ¡ENSÉÑAME DÓNDE ESTÁ MÚSICA Y YO TE AYUDARÉ A ENCONTRAR LO QUE HAS PERDIDO!

PERO... NO ES NECESARIO.

ESTOY BUSCANDO...

LO QUE BUSCO...

NO ES ALGO FÁCIL DE ENCONTRAR.

TE EQUIVOCAS...

...

MIS RECUER-DOS.

¿¡RECUER-DOS...!?

...

EM-PIEZAN HACE UN AÑO.

MIS RECUER-DOS...

CONFIANDO EN ENCONTRAR A ALGUIEN QUE ME CONOZCA.

POR ESO RECORRO EL MUNDO...

ESO TAMPOCO LO SÉ.

SLUMP

¿POR QUÉ NO TIENES RECUERDOS?

¿RE-CUER-DOS?

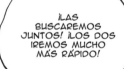

¡LAS BUSCAREMOS JUNTOS! ¡LOS DOS IREMOS MUCHO MÁS RÁPIDO!

DE REPENTE, VUELVEN A MÍ.

ALGUNAS VECES HE OLVIDADO COSAS, PERO...

...

CLASP

OH...

¿QUÉ DICES? ¡DEMON CARD YA NO ESTÁ, YA NO NECESITAMOS PAGARLES!

ES VERDAD...

NO TENEMOS DINERO PARA SALIR DE LA CIUDAD.

¿PERO QUÉ HAREMOS?

PERO ANTES DE IR A PUNK STREET...

¡PUES SALGAMOS DE LA CIUDAD!

¡ADELANTE!

CHA NK

CRICK

CRICK

CRICK

CRICK

KABOUMM

¡¡REMODELARÉ EL ESTADIO!!

CRICK

CRICK

2B

CRICK

CRICK

¿NO QUERÍAS DERRIBARLO?

¿CÓMO?

¿PERO QUÉ DICES? ¡NO ES LO QUE QUERÍA!

¡PARECE QUE AQUÍ HAY UNA SALIDA!

¡BUSQUEMOS UNA PUERTA Y LARGUÉMONOS!

¡ESTO ES MUY INESTABLE!

¡MIERDA! ¡ESTÁ A PUNTO DE DERRUMBARSE!

¡SÓLO QUEDA ESTA PUERTA!

FUOOOOO

RAPSODIA

FORTALEZA MIGRATORIA RAPSODIA, CONTINENTE SONG.

ESA BELLEZA ES DE NUESTRO GRUPO, PODEMOS DISPONER DE ELLA COMO QUERAMOS.

¡NO ME CANSO DE ELLA!

¿OTRA VEZ MIRANDO FOTOS DE REINA?

¿CÓMO DIRECTIVA? NO LO DICES EN SERIO.

Y PRONTO ESTARÁ EN LA CÚPULA DIRECTIVA.

¡NO HABLES DE ELLA CON ESA FALTA DE RESPETO! ¡LLÁMALA SEÑORA REINA!

FLAP

TAP

¿¡SEÑOR SHUDA!?

HAN DERROTADO A GEORCO.

¿QUÉ ESTARÁ HACIENDO HARU?

RECUPÉRALA.

PARECE QUE LE HAN QUITADO SU DARK BRING.

¡SÍ!

¿A GEORCO!?

AHÍ TENEMOS AL ESPADACHÍN LANCE...

PUNK STREET...

VA HACIA PUNK STREET.

RAVE: 9 ✚ EL LEGENDARIO HERRERO

PUNK STREET

PUNK STREET, LA CIUDAD MÁS IMPORTANTE DEDICADA A LAS ARMAS.

¡INCREÍBLE, TODO EL MUNDO LLEVA ARMAS!

OH, ¡CUÁNTO TIEMPO!

PUNK STREET

GROOO ! PUUN.

¡SU NA-RIZ...!

¡¡NO!!

ES LA CIUDAD MÁS PELIGROSA AL NORTE DEL CONTINENTE SONG.

¡¡CLARO, HARU!! CORAZÓN ♥

LO PRIMERO ES...

ANTES DE IR A NUESTRO DESTINO...

.VALE.

¡TE LLEVARÉ A UN BUEN SITIO!

JEJE

BUENO, MIENTRAS ESTÉ RICO, DA IGUAL.

¿QUÉ TIPO DE RESTAURANTE SERÁ? ¿CARNE? ¿PESCADO? ¿O DE FIDEOS? PERO ES UNA CHICA, ES CAPAZ DE LLEVARME A UNA HELADERÍA...

¿EL PRIMER SITIO?

¡ES EL PRIMER LUGAR AL QUE IR EN ESTA CIUDAD!

TAP TAP TAP

¡TACHÁN!

CASINO GORGEOUS TIME.

casino
GORGEOUS TIME

¡¡ESTO NO!!

¿EH? LO PRIMERO ES ECHAR UNAS PARTIDILLAS, ¿NO?

ZRISH

CASINO GORGEOUS TIME

OK!!

PLUE Y YO VAMOS A ESE RESTAURANTE.

AH, TENÉIS HAMBRE.

¡¡LO PRIMERO ES COMER!!

P.O Pastel

PaSta dinner&lu

ESTÁ COMO UNA REGADERA.

GROOOØ

CO... ¿COMANDANTE?

¡¡BIEN, COMANDANTE!! ¡¡CONSEGUIRÉ FONDOS PARA LA CAMPAÑA!!

JUHU

TRAPP TRAPP

POM

¿ES QUE NO HAY ALCOHOL EN ESTE TUGURIO?

HUM...

ZOO OM

¡¡LARGO, RÁPIDO!!

¿CUÁNTAS VECES TE LO HE DE DECIR!?

¡¡FUERA DE MI ESTABLECIMIENTO!!

PLUMPS

¡EN ESE CASO DÉJAMELO A MÍ!

¡¡JUA JUA JUA JUA JUA!!

¿¡CÓMO!?

TUIN TUIN TUIN TUIN TUIN-TUIN

JUA JUA JUA JUA

ESO QUIERE DECIR QUE...

¿SABE DÓNDE PUEDO ENCONTRAR A MÚSICA?

TUIN TUIN TUIN TUIN

JAMM

EXIT

JO... NO HAY MÁS REMEDIO.

QUIERO... VOLVER A CASA

PERO... NO PUEDO CAMINAR

CLAP CLAP CLAP

BOOOM

QUIERO... VOLVER A CASA...

¡JIA JIA JIA!

¿CUÁNDO ME VA A LLEVAR HASTA MÚSICA?

OIGA...

¡BIEN, CHICO! ¡BEBE, BEBE!

PUUN.

HNG HNG

BRR BRR

PUUN.

GNNNNN

ZACK

PUUN.

¡¡SE HA DORMIDO!!

HRRRRR CHRRRR HRRRRR

CLOC

PUUN.

ZUCK ZUCK

PLUE, ESTÁS BORRACHO.

PLUMP

ZACK

AHORA VERÁS...

¡JIA, JIA, JIA! ¡BIEN HECHO, CHICO!

CLANG

¡¡UAAAAH!!

ZAC

PLASSHHH

¡¡!!

¡COMO SE LE PASA LA BORRACHERA!

QUÉ CRÍO MÁS PESADO. DA GRACIAS QUE YA NO ESTOY BEBIDO.

DÍGAME DÓNDE ENCONTRAR A MÚSICA.

¡QUÉ FRÍA!

¿DE QUÉ VAS, CHAVAL?

SOY EL HERRERO MÚSICA.

PUES SÍ.

¡POR FIN LO ENCONTRÉ!

ES MÚSICA... EL LEGENDARIO HERRERO...

¿SHIBA? ¿SHIBA EL ESPADACHÍN? HACE MUCHO QUE NO SÉ DE ÉL...

PLONC

SHIBA, ME HABLÓ DE USTED.

SHSH

GRAD

VALE...

PUEDES QUEDARTE AQUÍ.

TAP TAP

¡¡GRA-CIAS!!

SEGURO QUE AÚN ESTÁ EN EL CASINO.

DOS DÍAS... TENGO QUE IR A POR ELIE.

RRR

ZAC

fiiiii

Gener

CHAC

HUM... ESTÁ SOBRE LA MESA.

TENGO LO QUE QUE-RÍAS.

ESO SIGNIFICA QUE EL CHICO TIENE RAVE...

NO ME HABLES CON ESOS AIRES, DESGRACIADO.

¡EL SEÑOR LANCE ESTARÁ MUY DISGUSTADO! ¡NO PODRÁS BEBER MÁS!

¡ESTO NO NOS SIRVE!

PRONTO SUPERARÁS ESTA MALA RACHA, YA VERÁS.

HOY TAMPOCO.

YA.

LA FORTUNA ES CAPRICHOSA.

ESO DICEN...

¡SEGURO QUE HARU SE ALEGRA CUANDO SEPA CUÁNTO HE GANADO!

¡¡HOY ESTOY DE SUERTE!!

RAVE: 10 ✠ EL DESCENSO DEL ÁNGEL ERRANTE.

ESTO...

...

¿ERES MÚSICA?

BASTA.

TAP
TAP

¿Y CÓMO SABES SU NOMBRE?

TÚ, ¿QUÉ QUIERES DE MÚSICA?

¿EH?

¡¡TE EQUI-VOCAS!!

NOOOOOOO

SEGURO QUE AHORA CAMBIA MI SUERTE.

¿QUÉ QUIERE DE MÍ UNA CHICA TAN GUAPA?

EXACTO.

ASÍ QUE ERES MÚSICA.

¿PUE-DES VENIR CON-MIGO?

QUIERO PEDIRTE UN FA-VOR...

¡OSTRAS!

ESTA CHICA TAN MONA... ¡MI SUERTE EMPIEZA A CAMBIAR!

NO HE GANADO NADA EN EL CASINO, PERO...

JE.

PUES... ¡PUES CLARO!

¡BIEN!

¿NO PUEDES?

ES QUE...

BUENO, GUAPA...

AQUÍ ESTÁS.

¡AH, HARU! ¡AQUÍ! ¡AQUÍ!

YA LE VALE A ESE MÚSICA. CUANDO VE A UNA CHICA GUAPA...

JU JU JU

¡CÁLLATE, BOCAZAS!

GRRR

BLA BLA

¡EH, CHICOS! ¡NOS VEMOS ESTA NOCHE EN LA SALA DE JUEGOS!

¡¡NO, ESPERAD!! ¡NOS VEMOS MAÑANA!

¿¡EH!?

SUPONGO QUE ES UNA CONFUSIÓN... YO BUSCABA AL HERRERO MÚSICA.

TÚ... ¿ERES UN LADRÓN?

¿CÓMO!?

LO SIENTO, PERO NI NOS SUENAS.

¡¡QUE NO!!

¿NO SERÁ UNA TROLA?

NO HE OÍDO HABLAR DE ÉL.

¿EL HERRERO MÚSICA?

SÍ, NO HAY DUDA.

?

¿ES ÉL?

ESTA CIUDAD TAN PELIGROSA ESTÁ LLENA DE ESBIRROS DE DEMON CARD.

¡TENED CUIDADO, QUE ES TARDE!

¡ADIÓS!

ES VERDAD, NO ES MÁS QUE UN CRÍO.

DEATH

¿QUÉ QUERÉIS?

!

ESOS TIPOS... ¿SON DE DEMON CARD?

JE JE

LAS NOTICIAS VUELAN...

¡TENDRÉIS QUE DARME BUENOS INCENTIVOS PARA QUE ME UNA A DEMON CARD!

¡AÚN VAIS A TENER QUE ESPERAR CIEN AÑOS!

!

...

CREO QUE ÉSTE NO ES EL CHICO.

DEATH

¡¡JA, JA, JA!! ¡NO TENGO NADA ROBADO!

¿ES VUESTRO JEFE?

¡¡ES EL FAMOSO LADRÓN SILVER RHYTHM!!

TRES PIERCINGS PLATEADOS EN LA FRENTE...

SEA COMO FUERE, ÚLTIMAMENTE HAY MUCHAS BANDAS DE JÓVENES QUE OPERAN POR DEBAJO DE DEMON CARD...

DEATH

HMM

¡¡ESE VIEJO!!

DEATH

ME LO TEMÍA.

¡¡SÍ!!

¡MATAD-LES!

¡AQUÍ OS QUEDÁIS!

QU... ¿¡QUÉ TE PA-SA!?

¡¡¡UAAH!!!

GÑÑÑ

¡ESTO ES TERRIBLE!

¿CREES QUE NOS LA PODRÍAMOS LLEVAR A ESPALDAS DEL JEFE?

SERÍA UNA PENA MATAR A LA CHICA.

NO ME PARECIÓ UN MENTIROSO.

PERO ESE HOMBRE ES MÚSICA

¿EN QUÉ ESTABA PENSANDO ESE DESGRACIADO DE MÚSICA!?

SI EL SUCESOR DE RAVE NO LA TIENE CONSIGO...

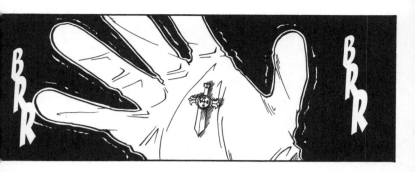

RAVE...

GLUC GLUC

CLASP

CLASP

¡NO ES DIGNO DE LLEVARLA!

ESE NIÑO TONTO...

RAVE: 11 ✛ DESDE LA PUERTA ROTA.

DEMON CARD, MANSIÓN DE LANCE.

DEMON CARD, MANSIÓN DE LANCE

SÍ, SEÑOR LANCE, PERO...

¿POR QUÉ BIS Y LOS SUYOS TARDAN TANTO?

QUIZÁ NO PUEDE CON EL SUCESOR...

ESTO... ES QUE...

ES SÓLO UNA IDEA.

¡TSK! ¡LE PASA POR ESTAR DEMASIADO GORDO!

¡NO LE DEFRAUDARÁ!

¡SEGURO QUE VOLVERÁ CON RAVE Y EL SUCESOR!

PRONTO SALDRÁ DE SU ESCONDRIJO.

PERO DA IGUAL. SI ÉSE ES EL CASO, YO ME DESHARÉ DE ÉL.

¡AÑADIRÉ ALGUNAS VÍCTIMAS MÁS A MI CUENTA!

DEMON CARD:
LANCE

SI ESE HOMBRE NO ES UN MENTIROSO, ENTONCES YO SÍ LO SOY. ¿EN QUÉ QUEDAMOS?

¿EH?

¿EIN?

PODRÍA SER...

¿NO PUEDE SER QUE HAYA DOS PERSONAS CON EL MISMO NOMBRE?

YO NO HE LLAMADO MENTIROSO A NADIE.

AHORA QUE LO DICES, NO LOS VEO.

¿DÓNDE ESTÁN PLUE Y ELIE?

ÉSTE NO ES UN BUEN SITIO PARA QUE UNA CHICA VAYA SOLA.

OYE... LOS DE DEMON CARD LA CONOCEN.

¿HABRÁ IDO A REPARAR LA GUN'S TONGFER?

DIJO QUE TENÍA QUE DEVOLVER UNA COSA.

¿NO ESTÁS PREOCUPADO?

NO HAY MUCHOS SITIOS DONDE REPARAR UNA GUN'S TONGFER.

¿POR QUÉ NO COMPRAS UNA NUEVA?

¡LE PAGARÉ EL DOBLE!

NO PUEDO. SEGÚN LA LEY, SI PASAN MÁS DE SEIS MESES DESDE SU ADQUISICIÓN, EL ARMA PIERDE LA GARANTÍA.

¡PERO TIENE QUE AYUDARME!

¡QUIERO ÉSTA!

?

¡BAH! ¡NO ES LA ÚNICA TIENDA!

SOY EL COMANDANTE DE LA DECIMOSÉPTIMA DIVISIÓN DE DEMON CARD...

JU...

¿SERÁ DE DEMON CARD?

¿QUIÉN ERES?

¡NO LO OLVIDES!

EL ESPADACHÍN LANCE.

O SI NO LA MATARÉ.

TIENES DOS HORAS, HASTA LAS CINCO, PARA LLEVARME A RAVE A MI MANSIÓN.

ANTES DAME A RAVE.

¡¡SUELTA A ELIE!!

¡ESO, SUÉLTAME!

ENTONCES VE A BUSCARLA.

NO LA TENGO.

UGH UGH

SI TARDAS UN SÓLO MINUTO MÁS...

ESTA CHICA MORIRÁ.

DOMM

UOOOA

¡¡SUELTA A ELIE!!

BUOFF

¡TENDRÁS QUE SEPARARTE UN RATO DE TU AMORCITO!

SKSSH

TIENES DOS HORAS PARA CALMARTE.

VOY A TOMAR POSICIONES JUNTO A SU CASA.

¡¡MALDITO DESGRACIADO!!

HA HUIDO...

¡VE A BUSCAR A RAVE, RÁPIDO!

...

ESTOY... PREOCUPADO POR ELIE.

¿POR QUÉ QUIERES AYUDARME?

CASI NO NOS CONOCEMOS...

OYE...

¿CÓ-
MO...?

¡NO HA
MUERTO!
¡SOY SU
SUCESOR!

ESO
QUIERE DE-
CIR QUE...
¿SHIBA HA
MUERTO?

VAYA...
TÚ ERES EL
MAESTRO DE
RAVE...

JE
JE

¡TIENE
QUE RE-
PARAR LA
ESPADA
EN ME-
NOS DE
DOS
HORAS!

DEJE
ESO, ¡HAN
SECUES-
TRADO A
MI AMIGA!

?

SE
EQUIVO-
CA.

AHORA NO
SOY MÁS
QUE UN
BORRACHO,
UN PELELE
DE DEMON
CARD.

¿NO TE HAS
DADO CUENTA?
HE DEJADO LA
HERRERÍA.

GLUG
GLUG
GLUG

ZRISH

EL HOMBRE QUE POSEE LA ÚLTIMA ESPADA DEL HERRERO "MÚSICA"...

¡¡¡LANCE!!!

¿IVAS A ENFRENTARTE A LANCE!?

¿LO DICES EN SERIO?

ESTE NIÑO...

ESO VOY A HACER.

SÍ.

140

PERO... ¿¡QUÉ ESTÁ HACIENDO!?

DODOM DODOM

PLOP

NO QUERÍA RECORDAR.

FU OO A

SPLASH

PERO AHORA HAY ALGO QUE PUEDO HACER PARA COMBATIR.

ASÍ QUE ME PERDÍ EN LA BOTELLA Y ME CONVERTÍ EN UN PELELE DE DEMON CARD.

HASTA AHORA, CREÍA QUE NO HABÍA NADA QUE PUDIERA HACER.

142

RAVE: 12 ✚ EL SUCESOR

EN ESTE ESTADO, ROTA, ESTA ESPADA NECESITARÍA UNO O DOS DÍAS PARA REPARARSE.

NO TENGAS TANTA PRISA, HAN PASADO 15 AÑOS...

AH, AQUÍ.

MÚSICA... ¿LE DARÁ TIEMPO?

FSSSSH

¡ÑÑÑ!

¡NO VOLVERÁ A ROMPERSE, EL NERVIO ES MÁS FUERTE!

¡TRANQUILO, LLEGARÁS A TIEMPO!

¡PERO SI ANTES ME DIJO QUE PODRÍA HACERLO!

SI NO SE DA PRISA, ELIE...

PERO ÉSTA ES UNA REPARACIÓN DE UNA HORA...

ESO

144

FUOOO

FUO OOO

ESO ES.

¿EL NER-VIO?

¡ESO FUNCIONA CON LAS ARMAS Y LAS PERSO-NAS!

¡CON ESTA FUERTE GUÍA, NO SE ROMPE-RÁ!

FUO OO

¡EL NERVIO ES FUER-TE!

¡MENOS LA NARIZ DE PLUE!

GRRRR

PUUN.

BRR

BRR

SÓLO QUEDA MEDIA HORA PARA LAS CINCO.

¿PERO QUÉ ESTÁ HACIENDO?

¿QUÉ ESTÁS HACIENDO AQUÍ?

!

HE QUE-DADO.

EN FIN, NOS VE-REMOS DENTRO, HARU.

AAAH AAH

UAAAH

!

¡¡UN INTRUSO!!

TSK.

FUOOOO

ES... ¡SILVER RHYTHM MÚSICA!

NO SERÁ QUE... ¿VIENES A LIQUI-DAR-NOS?

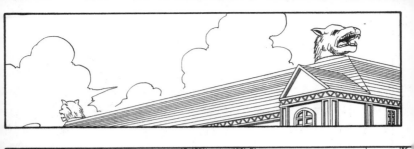

FUOOOOOOO

SILVER
RHYTHM
MÚSICA...

ES
TERRI-
BLE...

AH
AH

UFF
UFF

OIGA.

GRRR

TAP
TAP

GRRR
GRRR

¿POR QUÉ PASA DE MÍ?

DIJO QUE JUGARÍAMOS A LAS ADIVINANZAS.

CLLIN NG

VALE, PUES EMPIEZO YO.

VEAMOS...

PLATA PARECE, ORO NO ES...

LO SIENTO.

GRRR

¡ERES IRRITANTE!

ESTOY HARTA DE ESTA POSTURA.

PUES...

¿EH?

PERO TÚ... ¿NO ESTÁS PREOCUPADA POR TU SITUACIÓN?

!

¡AH!

HUM

VEO QUE NO HAS TENIDO PROBLEMAS EN LLEGAR...

CHAC

ELIE, NO TE HABRÁ HECHO NADA RARO, ¿NO?

¡NO ES MOMENTO PARA TUS BROMITAS!

GRRR

¿¡CÓMO!?

PAM

¡SÍ! ¡ME HA TOCADO EL PECHO!

...

BUH

NO TE LO SABRÍA DECIR.

¡NO ME ENFADES MÁS AÚN!

FRISH

¿DÓNDE ESTÁ EL MAESTRO RAVE?

Y ENTONCES...

¿HUM?

DEATH

¡ACABO DE REGRESAR Y ME HE ENCONTRADO CON TODOS NUESTROS HOMBRES FUERA DE COMBATE!

¡¡SEÑOR LANCE!! ¿¡QUÉ HA OCURRIDO!?

TAP   TAP

¿DÓNDE TE HABÍAS METIDO?

¿¡O SEA QUE HAS SIDO TÚ!?

MIERDA...

ZAS ZAS

¡PERO BUENO! ¡SI ERES EL CHICO DE ANTES!

¿LO ENTENDÉIS?

FUI A CASA DEL VIEJO, PORQUE PENSABA QUE ENCONTRARÍA A RAVE, PERO ME DERROTARON... HE VENIDO EN BUSCA DE ALGÚN ARMA...

FRISH

BASTA, BIS.

ENCÁRGATE DE ESTE CHICO.

ZU

M

DEATH

¿HUM?

¿QUIERES QUE ME CARGUE AL GORDITO?

ZUCK

¡SÍ, ENSE-GUIDA!

¡TÚ! ¡TRÁEME EL CLAN KEYMAN!

OH... ¡¡ENTEN-DIDO!!

¡SE HA PA-SA-DO!

¡EL SEÑOR BIS NO SO-PORTA ESA PALA-BRA!

¡ESTÁ MUER-TO!

CÓMO... ¿¡CÓMO ACABAS DE LLAMAR-ME!?

RRRR

FSSSSH

NO HAS SIDO MUY EDUCA-DO.

CLAC

NO... LA VER-DAD ES QUE NO.

¿Y QUÉ TAL CER-DO?

¿NO TE GUSTA "GORDITO"?

JI JI JI

¡¡TE MATARÉ!!

¿¡QUÉ ES ESO!? ¡LE SALE HUMO!

PUUUH

FIUUUUUU

¡AHORA VERÁS EL TERRIBLE PODER DEL CLAN KEYMAN!

¡TE HARÉ PICADILLO!

ERES MUY ABURRIDO.

POOO OM

¡¡GÑÑ!

JU...

QUÉ INTERESANTE...

¡¡HIIII!!

¡HACE QUE EL CLAN KEYMAN DEL SEÑOR BIS PAREZCA UN JUGUETE!

¿CÓMO LO HACE!?

¡¡MÚSICA ERES FANTÁSTICO!!

!!

¡¡¡UAAAGHHH!!!

SLASH

SUPONGO QUE LO HABRÍAS MATADO.

...ERA TU COMPAÑERO...

MAL-DI-TO...

NO PARECES AFECTA-DO.

MÁS BIEN UN PEÓN.

¿COMPA-ÑERO?

ES QUE TENGO QUE IR CALENTANDO LA ESPADA.

DESPUÉS DE QUE LANCE ASESINARA A LOS MÍOS, NO ME QUEDÓ NINGUNA ESPERANZA.

¿A QUÉ VIENE ESO...?

YO... ANTES DE DEJAR LA HERRERÍA, ERA FELIZ CON MI FAMILIA.

HA-RU...

?

¿DE VE-RAS!?

¿CÓ-MO...!?

LANCE MATÓ A MI FAMILIA CON LA ESPADA QUE FORJÉ.

HGH

CLANG CLANG CLANG PFFT

...

MI ES-PA-DA LOS MA-TÓ...

MI ES-PA-DA...

CLINNNG

¡¡PUUN!!

¡¡PUUN!!

YA PUEDES LLE-VÁR-TE-LA.

AQUÍ TIENES LA ESPA-DA.

BRR

BRR

BRR

¡¡PUUN!!

RAVE: 13 ✚ EL PUENTE DE LA PROMESA

¿EMPEZAMOS O QUÉ?

BIEN...

HACÍA MUCHO QUE NO ME HERÍAN.

USAS LAS ILUSIONES PARA DESPISTAR AL ADVERSARIO...

YA LO ENTIENDO...

?

ENTONCES YO TAMBIÉN ME PONDRÉ SERIO.

¿ASÍ QUE ESTO NO HA SIDO MÁS QUE UN NUMERITO?

JU... LA HERIDA CADA VEZ ES MÁS GRANDE, ESTÚPIDO.

UGH...

¿QUÉ ES LO QUE DICES!?

AGH...

!?

NO ME APETECE.

QUÉ
PESA-
DO...

UGH...

FRFRFR

¡¡DETENTE!!

EL
MOMENTO
DE MATAR.

HE
TENIDO QUE
ESPERAR
MUCHO ESTE
MOMENTO.

FUOOOO

¡¡¡¡HARU!!!!

¡MUERE!

FUU

MM

HEART KREUZ

CRRRI

¿ESTÁS
BIEN,
ELIE?

ii...!!

TE ESTABA ESPERANDO, MAESTRO RAVE.

JU...

¡SE HA DESHECHO DE LA ESPADA DEL SEÑOR LANCE!

HAS PUESTO A ELIE EN PELIGRO.

NO PIENSO PERDONÁRTELO.

PULUN.

BRR
BRR
BRR

¡GRACIAS POR VENIR TÚ TAMBIÉN, PLUE! ♡

SHAK

VAYA... ¿ES LA FAMOSA ESPADA DE LOS DIEZ PODERES?

HARU... YO LO MATARÉ.

HACÍA MUCHO QUE NO ME TOPABA CON ALGUIEN DE MI NIVEL.

DEBO SER YO QUIEN LO DERROTE.

NO.

¿CÓMO!?

...

DEBO DESTRUIRLO...

SE LO HE PROMETIDO AL OTRO MÚSICA, EL HERRERO.

NO...

¡DEBO DESTRUIR ESA ESPADA!

CLASP

BAFF

¿ASÍ QUE QUIERES MATAR-ME?

SHA

KK

DEJAD YA DE PARLO-TEAR.

...

¡¡BES-
TIAS
IMAGI-
NARIAS!!

TAPP

¡¡IDIOTA!!
¡NO VAYAS
HACIA ÉL!

¡ESA
TÉCNI-
CA!

¿¡¡QUÉ!!?

SHAASH

CLANNNG

BUOff

UGH...

¡LAS ILUSIONES HAN DESAPARECIDO!

TE DIRÉ CÓMO DERROTAR A ESA ESPADA.

BESTIAS IMAGINA-RIAS.

LA ESPADA QUE GENERA...

LAS ILUSIONES SÓLO APARE-CEN CUANDO LA ESPADA APUNTA HACIA ABAJO.

¡¡GENIAL!!

*BRR

¡PUUN!

BRR

...

¡¡ESA TÉCNICA NO FUNCIONA!!

ASÍ QUE, SI DETENGO LA ESPADA ANTES DE QUE DESCRIBA EL ARCO DESCENDENTE...

GÑÑ GÑÑ

ZRISH

PERO...

SHKK

JU, JU, JU... VEO QUE HAS HECHO LOS DEBERES.

CAPÍTULOS EDITADOS POR PRIMERA VEZ EN LA REVISTA SHUKAN SHONEN MAGAZINE DEL AÑO 1999, DEL

SEGURO QUE NO CONOCES TODAS LAS TÉCNICAS DE ESTA ESPADA.

FUO

OOOO

¿ES OTRA ILUSIÓN DE LA ESPADA?

PERO... ¿¡QUÉ ES ESO!?

CONTINUARÁ...

PÁGINA EXTRA

¡MUCHAS GRACIAS POR VUESTRAS CARTAS!
ESTOY MUY EMOCIONADO. ANTES DE EMPEZAR LA
SERIE, PENSABA RESPONDER A TODAS LAS CARTAS
QUE ME ENVIARAN LOS FANS, PERO HAY DEMASIADAS...
HE RECIBIDO MUCHAS MÁS DE LAS QUE IMAGINABA,
Y COMO ESTOY TAN OCUPADO DIBUJANDO LA SERIE
(QUE SE PUBLICA SEMANALMENTE EN JAPÓN) ME ES
IMPOSIBLE RESPONDERLAS. LO SIENTO MUCHO. PERO
ESO SÍ, LAS LEO TODAS. ME DAN MUCHOS ÁNIMOS.
SON MI TESORO MÁS PRECIADO.
SIEMPRE QUE TENGO UN DESCANSO, PIENSO EN
DEDICAR UN RATO A RESPONDERLAS. ASÍ QUE, EN
DEFINITIVA, OS AGRADEZCO MUCHO VUESTRO APOYO.

HIRO MASHIMA.

ELIE: LA CHICA SIN RECUERDOS

G'TONGFER
(GUN'S TONGFER)
MODELO
M-644.
COMPRADA
EN PUNK
STREET.

ARMAS: G'TONGFER
ANIVERSARIO/EDAD: DESCONOCIDO/
DESCONOCIDO (DEBE DE TENER
UNOS 16 AÑOS)
ALTURA/PESO/GRUPO SANGUÍNEO: 160 CM/
45 KG/ DESCONOCIDO (QUIZÁ EL O)

NACIÓ EN: DESCONOCIDO
AFICIONES: JUGAR CON PLUE, IR DE COMPRAS
HABILIDADES: LOS JUEGOS DE AZAR
(TIENE MUCHA SUERTE)
COSAS QUE APRECIA: HEART KREUZ
LOVE BELIEVER (TANTO EL CONCEPTO
COMO LA MARCA DE ROPA)

COSAS QUE TEME:
LOS TRUENOS

CAMISETA
(HEART
KREUZ)

CINTURÓN DE
G'TONGFER (DE
LOVE BELIEVER)

MINIFALDA
DENIM

LLEVA UN
BRAZALETE DE
LOVE BELIEVER
Y LLEVA UN
COLGANTE EN
FORMA DE
CORAZÓN
(SIN MARCA).

BOTAS
ALTAS

AL FINAL ME HA SALIDO UN PERSONAJE
CON ALGO DE MALA LECHE. PERO ESO
SÍ, ME HE DIVERTIDO DIBUJÁNDOLA. ESTÁ
SIEMPRE PREPARADA PARA TODO Y SE
MUEVE CON MUCHA LIBERTAD.
NO RECUERDA NADA DE SU PASADO.
NO ES UN PERSONAJE MUY ORIGINAL,
PERO ME GUSTAN MUCHO LOS MISTERIOS
Y TENÍA GANAS DE CREAR A ALGUIEN
SIN PASADO. ¡¡PERDÓNAME, ELIE!!
¿NO OS PREGUNTÁIS CÓMO HA SIDO
SU PASADO? (RISAS) PUES HABLANDO
DE TODO UN POCO, AÚN NO LO HE
DECIDIDO. BUENO, ELIE... ES QUE...

EL LOGO DE HEART KREUZ.
ESA PALABRA, HEART KREUZ,
ESTÁ FORMADA POR CORAZÓN Y
UNA CRUZ. ES UNA MARCA MUY
POPULAR ENTRE LAS CHICAS.

EL HERRERO LEGENDARIO: MÚSICA

ARMAS: MARTILLO DE HIERRO
EDAD/ANIVERSARIO: 4 DE OCTUBRE DE 1998/ 70 AÑOS
ALTURA/PESO/GRUPO SANGUÍNEO: 171 CM/ 62 KG/B
NACIÓ EN: PUNK STREET

AFICIONES: LA BEBIDA
HABILIDADES: ES EL MEJOR
FORJADOR DE ESPADAS DEL MUNDO
COSAS QUE APRECIA:
LOS QUE BEBEN ALCOHOL
COSAS QUE DESPRECIA: LANCE

ME COSTÓ BASTANTE DIBUJAR
A ESTE PERSONAJE. ME INSPIRÉ
EN UN HERRERO QUE VI EN UNA
PELÍCULA, Y ÉSTA ES LA IMPRESIÓN
QUE ME DIO. SE DEDICA A BEBER
COMO UN COSACO...
¡Y NO SE OS OCURRA BEBER
HASTA QUE NO SEÁIS MAYORES
DE EDAD!

¡SE LLAMA MÚSICA, COMO
LA PALABRA ITALIANA PARA
MELODÍA! ASÍ QUE...

← ÉSTE ES SU
SÍMBOLO.

EL JEFE DE LAS CARRERAS DE PERROS: GEORCO

ARMAS: SU BASTÓN Y DARK BRING (LO CONVIERTE EN HUMO)
ANIVERSARIO/EDAD: 14 DE MARZO DE 0026/ 40 AÑOS
ALTURA/PESO/GRUPO SANGUÍNEO: 142 CM/ 40 KG/ O
NACIÓ EN: HIP HOP TOWN

AFICIONES: BURLARSE DE SUS SUBORDINADOS
HABILIDADES: BEBER LECHE RÁPIDAMENTE
COSAS QUE APRECIA: EL DINERO Y LAS COSAS BRILLANTES
COSAS QUE DESPRECIA: LOS QUE INTERFIEREN EN SUS CARRERAS

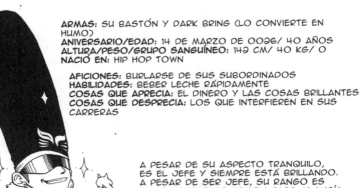

A PESAR DE SU ASPECTO TRANQUILO, ES EL JEFE Y SIEMPRE ESTÁ BRILLANDO. A PESAR DE SER JEFE, SU RANGO ES BAJO DENTRO DE DEMON CARD, Y ANSÍA OCUPAR UN PUESTO MÁS IMPORTANTE DENTRO DE LA ORGANIZACIÓN. PERO SU TÉCNICA DEL HUMO PARECE BASTANTE PODEROSA... ¡NO! ¡ESO NO ES VERDAD! NO PUEDE LUCHAR EN DÍAS DE VIENTO, Y TAMPOCO TIENE MUCHA EXPERIENCIA EN LA LUCHA. POR ESO SU RANGO ES BAJO EN DEMON CARD. ES SÓLO UN JEFE INTERMEDIO.

¡ÉSTA ES LA MARCA DE DEMON CARD! LA VERDAD ES QUE SÓLO MODIFIQUÉ LAS LETRAS DC...

AL FINAL LA IMAGEN ES COMO DOS ALAS. ¡SIMBOLIZA QUE DC SE EXTIENDE POR TODO EL MUNDO!

COMANDANTE DE LA DECIMOSÉPTIMA DIVISIÓN DE DEMON CARD: EL ESPADACHÍN LANCE

ARMAS: SU ESPADA (BESTIAS IMAGINARIAS) Y DARK BRING (REAL MOMENT)
ANIVERSARIO/EDAD: 6 DE FEBRERO DE 0028/ 38 AÑOS
ALTURA/PESO/GRUPO SANGUÍNEO: 218 CM/ 97 KG/A
NACIÓ EN: BLUES CITY
AFICIONES: MATAR GENTE
HABILIDADES: NO SE HA LICENCIADO, PERO TIENE HABILIDADES DE VETERINARIO
COSAS QUE APRECIA: LAS FRESAS
COSAS QUE DESPRECIA: A LOS ESTÚPIDOS

HUM... BUENO, ES EL MALO. (¿ES OBVIO, NO?) HACÍA TIEMPO QUE TENÍA EN MENTE CREAR UN PERSONAJE QUE SE LLAMARA LANCE, PERO EN PRINCIPIO IBA A SER UN PERSONAJE CÓMICO. PERO CREAR UN PERSONAJE DE ESAS CARACTERÍSTICAS ES MUY COMPLICADO, Y SE TRANSFORMÓ EN ESTE TÍO TAN MALO.

MI PRIMER DISEÑO...

ESTE TIPO... ES DEMASIADO ABSURDO, ¿NO?

LEVIN QUEDA A CARGO DEL HOGAR. CAPÍTULO 2: PAPÁ Y MAMÁ

BUENO, ¿QUÉ SON?

BIEN... EN REALIDAD NO HABRÍA QUE LLAMARLOS PERSONAS...

SU-PON-GO...

Y DIME, ¿QUÉ TIPO DE PERSONAS SON?

ASÍ ES.

DIME, NAKAJIMA, ¿TIENES PAPÁ Y MAMÁ?

¡¡RES-PONDE A MI PRE-GUNTA!!

Y SON PEGA-JO-SOS...

¡ESO NO ES LO QUE QUERÍA SABER!

Y TAMBIÉN CANTAN.

JA JA

¡ES LO QUE MÁS LES GUS-TA!

¡LES EN-CANTA EL RA-MEN!

¡¡PAPÁ, MAMÁ, VOLVED PRON-TO!!

¿QUÉ ES ESTA SOMBRA TAN SOSPECHOSA!?

NO LES PAGAN MU-CHO, PERO ES UN BUEN TRA-BAJO.

¿¡CÓMOOOO!?

SON ES-CA-RA-BA-JOS.

AHORA MISMO TE LO DIGO.

¡ESO, SU TRA-BAJO!

¡SU TRA-BAJO! ¡QUIERO SABER A QUÉ SE DEDI-CAN!

¿HABRÁ TERCER CAPÍTULO?

HIRO MASHIMA Y SUS AYUDANTES

AUTORRETRATO

H
U
M
...

ZU MM

DATOS

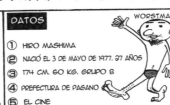

WORSTMAN

① HIRO MASHIMA

② NACIÓ EL 3 DE MAYO DE 1977. 27 AÑOS

③ 174 CM. 60 KG. GRUPO B

④ PREFECTURA DE PAGANO

⑤ EL CINE

⑥ CORTARSE EL PELO
(ESTE AÑO SE LO HA CORTADO ÉL MISMO TRES VECES)

⑦ ¡POR SUPUESTO, SUS FANS!

⑧ ¿LAS ORUGAS!

CREO QUE LA ILUSTRACIÓN DE LA IZQUIERDA SE LE PARECE BASTANTE, ¿NO? ESTE AÑO HE CAMBIADO MUCHO DE COLOR DE PELO: DE NEGRO A RUBIO Y AHORA LO TENGO ENTRE RUBIO Y PLATEADO. ¡SI VEO UNA ORUGA, SOY INCAPAZ DE TOCARLA!

DATOS

① KOJI NAKAMURA

② 11 DE SEPTIEMBRE DE 1976

③ 156 CM. 50 KG. GRUPO A

④ PREFECTURA DE FUKUOKA

⑤ COMER PLÁTANOS

⑥ COMER PLÁTANOS

⑦ PLÁTANOS

⑧ ¡NO PODER COMER PLÁTANOS!

⑨ ¡¡COMAMOS PLÁTANOS!!

¡MASHIMA ES EL MÁS RARO DE TODOS! NO ES ASÍ, EXACTAMENTE...

RAMEN TAILANDÉS.

Y AQUÍ, LOS TRES ASISTENTES... UNAS PALABRAS DE MASHIMA.

PRINCIPALMENTE ME AYUDA A HACER LOS FONDOS. ES UN TIPO RARO. HACE LO QUE LE DIGO, AÚN NO ME HA DICHO NUNCA "NO QUIERO HACERLO". Y ADEMÁS... ¡LE GUSTAN LOS PLÁTANOS!

DATOS

① TETSUYA YAMAUE

② 21 DE JULIO DE 1977

③ 177 CM, 75 KG, GRUPO A

④ OSAKA

⑤ TODAS LAS COSAS INTERESANTES.

⑥ APRENDER COSAS INÚTILES.

⑦ LAS POLILLAS

⑧ AHORA LE HA DADO POR HABLAR CON ACENTO DE OSAKA

POM

I'M A FALLING ANGEL

LE LLAMAMOS YAMA. ME AYUDA CON LOS FONDOS Y LOS BLANCOS DE LA SERIE. SOLEMOS ENFRENTARNOS EN COMBATES A VIDEOJUEGOS. TAMBIÉN ES UN POCO RARITO. ES MUY ESPONTÁNEO. ¡Y ADEMÁS, SABE UN MONTÓN DE COSAS INÚTILES!

DATOS

ZZzz...

① YUKA T

② NACIÓ EL 2 DE SEPTIEMBRE DE 1977

③ 160 CM. GORDA. GRUPO O

④ IBARAKI

⑤ TEÑIRSE EL PELO. (AHORA ES BLANCO)

⑥ QUEJARSE POR TODO

⑦ LOS ANIMALES (HÁMSTERES, GATOS... VACAS...)

⑧ ODIO LAS COSAS ODIOSAS

⑨ QUIERO TENER UN HÁMSTER

MIAU

SU CARA EN EL CUERPO DE MI GATO.

YUKA ES LA QUE DA LOS TOQUES FINALES. ES LA ÚNICA CHICA. SIEMPRE TIENE ALGO QUE DECIR SOBRE LA ROPA DE LAS CHICAS, ¡DIBUJA LO QUE QUIERE! ¡SIEMPRE SE ESTÁ QUEJANDO POR TODO! ES, DE LEJOS, LA MÁS RARA DE TODOS MIS ASISTENTES. ¡PERO ESO HACE QUE EL TRABAJO SEA MUY DIVERTIDO!

LEYENDA DE LOS DATOS: 1. NOMBRE 2. ANIVERSARIO Y EDAD 3. ALTURA, PESO Y GRUPO SANGUÍNEO 4. LUGAR DE NACIMIENTO

POSTSCRIPT

¡COLEGUILLAS! SOY MASHIMA. COMO NO SÉ CUÁNDO LEERÉIS ESTO, SI POR LA MAÑANA, AL MEDIODÍA, POR LA TARDE O POR LA NOCHE, HE INVENTADO ESTE NUEVO SALUDO, PARA QUEDAR BIEN. ES MUY ÚTIL, PORQUE ASÍ NO IMPORTA CUÁNDO LO DIGAS, SIEMPRE ACIERTAS.

EL SEGUNDO VOLUMEN DE RAVE HA SALIDO RÁPIDAMENTE. ¡¡YUHU!! Y YA HAY 350 PÁGINAS DE MANGA... ¡PERO MI OBJETIVO SON UNOS DIEZ TOMOS! O POR LO MENOS ESO ES LO QUE CREO, CON LOS RUMORES... ¡SEGURO QUE LO CONSIGO, NO TENGO QUE AMILANARME! ¡¡LO CONSEGUIRÉ!! (SOY MUY INSISTENTE)

ESTE SEGUNDO TOMO, DE LOS CAPÍTULOS 5 A 13 HA SIDO COMPLICADO, PORQUE HE TENIDO QUE DISEÑAR EL ESTADIO Y LAS CIUDADES, QUE SIEMPRE DAN TRABAJO, Y ADEMÁS CON TANTA GENTE EXTRA, YO LO HE DIBUJADO CASI TODO. HA SIDO DURO, PERO LA VERDAD ES QUE MUY DIVERTIDO (RISAS). Y SOBRE TODO, CADA VEZ QUE DIBUJABA UNA PORTADILLA, ME DIVERTÍA MUCHO PENSANDO QUE ROPA LLEVARÍAN HARU Y SUS AMIGOS. EN LA PORTADILLA DEL CAPÍTULO 6 LE PUSE A HARU UN CINTURÓN DE LA MARCA OWNER LOVELY... UNA DERIVACIÓN DE OWNER LOVE... ONNA LOVE ("ONNA" ES MUJER EN JAPONÉS) ¿A QUE ES CURIOSO? ¡NOS VEMOS EN EL TERCER VOLUMEN! TENGO SUEÑO, VOY A DORMIR. BUENAS NOCHES.

HIRO
MASHIMA.

¡ATENCIÓN!

¡Este manga está publicado en el mismo sentido de lectura que la edición japonesa!

Tienes que empezar a leer por la que sería la última página de un libro occidental y seguir las viñetas de derecha a izquierda.

Rave nº2
Título original: "RAVE volume 2"
© 1999 Hiro Mashima. All Rights Reserved.
First published in Japan in 1999 by Kodansha., Ltd.,Tokyo.
Spanish publication rights arranged by Kodansha., Ltd.
© 2004 NORMA Editorial por la edición en castellano.
Passeig Sant Joan 7, principal. 08010 Barcelona.
Tel.: 93 303 68 20. – Fax: 93 303 68 31.
norma@normaeditorial.com

Traducción: Annabel Espada.
Rotulación: Xavier Amigó.
Depósito legal: B-02311-2004.
ISBN: 84-96325-25-3.
Printed in the EU.

www.NormaEditorial.com